Albert Kaganovich

The Mashhadi Jews (Djedids)
in Central Asia

Contents

The Mashhadi Jews (Djedids) in Central Asia	1
Djedid Settlements in Central Asia and Their Population	8
Legal Status in the Transcaspian oblast until Year 1917	30
Socio-Economic Life	45
Communal and Religious Life	59
Summary	70
Bibliography	73

Figures

Illustration 1: An old Herati Jew	iv
Table 1. Djedid population in the Transcaspian oblast in 1902 according to their citizenship	18
Table 2. Djedid population in the Transcaspian oblast in 1910 according to their citizenship	20
Illustration 2: Advertisements	71
Illustration 3: Turkmens	72

Illustration 1: An old Herati Jew. In: Weissenberg S., Die zentralasiatischen Juden in anthropologischer Beziehung, Wien, 1913, p. 260

Mashhad, the center of Khorasan, always has been one of the towns most revered by Shi'ites because the shrine of Imam Riza is situated there. Jews lived in the town until the beginning of the 18th century.[1] It is most likely that the Jews left Mashhad because of the growing religious fanaticism of the Moslem inhabitants. Wishing to develop the town's trade and crafts in the 1730s and in the 1740s, Nāder Shāh Afshār (1736-1747) again brought the Jews of Qazvin and other Iranian towns to Mashhad. This was opposed by the religious establishment of Iran, but the ruler prevailed.[2] The largest number of Jews came from Gilan province, and so the Gilaki dialect of Persian became the principal language of Mashhad Jews.[3] At the same time there was also another dialect spoken. It was Yazd dialect, brought here by a part of the Jewish immigrants.[4] After resettlement, many Jews started trading with Turkmenian tribes,[5] the ones living in the south of Turkmenia – Tekkes, Sālors and Saryks. Joseph Wolff, an English Protestant missionary of Jewish origin, who settled in Mashhad in 1831, claimed the local Jews even went to Russia for commerce with their caravans.[6] Lieutenant Colonel Johann Blaramberg, a Holland-born employee of the Russian government who visited Mashhad in 1838 as a member of a Russian delegation, pointed out that the main occupation of local Jews was trading in turquoise, which they themselves polished and

---

[1] Fischel, 1982, pp. 285-286.
[2] Levi believes that the migration occurred in 1730 and Fischel formerly believed that it had not come about until 1734, but later he came to the conclusion that it had happened during the reign of Nadir Shah. Ben-Zvi, in turn, thought it dated back to 1743, and Raphael Patai – to 1747. See: Ben-Zvi, 1966, p. 320; Fischel, 1936, pp. 49-51; Fischel, 1949, p. 28; Levy, 1980, p. 57; Patai, 1997, pp. 25-26.
[3] Netser, 1990, p. 137; Kupovetskiy, 1992, p. 62.
[4] Netser, 1990, p. 137; Kupovetskiy, 1992, p. 62; Dilmanian, 1997, pp. 15-16.
[5] Fischel, 1936, p. 52; Levy, 1987, p. 60; Wolff, 1837, p. 98. The squabble between a Moslem beggar and a Jew described by Arthur Conolly, evidences the trade Mashhadi Jews had with Turkmens, and Iranian slaves in particular. See: Conolly, 1834, vol. 1, p. 252 - 253.
[6] Wolff, 1837, p. 115.

set. Their jewelry was exported to Russia via Bukhara, and, to a lesser extent, to India.[7] Another English Protestant missionary of Jewish origin, Jacob Samuel, who visited Persia in 1836, wrote about a large number of Jews in Turkmenia (of whom he had heard),[8] obviously referring to the ones from Mashhad. The economic status of the Mashhadi Jews gradually improved, which drew Jews of other Iranian towns to settle there.[9]

Statistic information about Mashhadi Jews are somewhat contradictory. In 1807, the French officer M. Truilhier found only about 100 Jewish families in Mashhad,[10] while Georg Meyendorf, a Russian officer of German origin, learned from Jews of Bukhara that in 1821, the Mashhadi Jews had owned 300 houses.[11] Johann Blaramberg testified that in 1838, about 400 Jews lived there,[12] probably meaning the number of families. If we assume that, on average, five people lived in a Mashhadi house, similar to other homes in Central Asia,[13] the total number of Jews must have been two thousand. This is how Joseph Wolff estimated their population when he visited Mashhad again in 1843-1844.[14] Taking into consideration what happened to them in 1839 (see below) the statistics provided by Joseph Wolff seem to be somewhat overstated at the time of his second visit to Mashhad and probably his estimation corresponds more to the late 1830s. Against this background, the data provided by the following colonels seem to be greatly understated: the English colonel Arthur Conolly counted only 100 houses of Mashhadi

---

[7] Blaramberg, 1853, p. 235.
[8] Samuel, 1840, p. 11.
[9] Levy, 1980, p. 60.
[10] Ibid; Patai, 1997, p. 32.
[11] Meyendorf, 1826, p. 173.
[12] Blaramberg, 1853, p. 235.
[13] For the average number of residents in a house in Central Asia at that time see: Iavorskiy, 1889, p. 329.
[14] Wolff, vol. 1, 1860, p. 510.

Jews in 1831,[15] and the French colonel Joseph Ferrier mentioned that in 1845 there were only 600 Jews there.[16]

By the end of the 19th century, small Jewish communities existed in other towns of Khorasan as well: Kalat-e Naderi,[17] Sabzawar,[18] Nishapur and Turbat-i-Haidariyeh.[19] According to Wolff, there was a settlement of Mashhadi Jews in the Afghan town of Maimana.[20] During the first third of the 19th century, the economic status of the Mashhad Jews deteriorated as a result of increased persecutions and legal restrictions.[21] James Fraser, an English traveler who visited Mashhad in 1821, wrote about them: "...the miserable way common to this oppressed and ill-used class of men".[22] Jacob Samuel, the above-mentioned missionary, visited Persia in 1836 and wrote about the hard life of Jews in Persia in general.[23] The above-mentioned lieutenant colonel J.F. Blaramberg wrote several years later about the attitude towards Mashhadi Jews and about their occupation: "Kikes ...are disregarded by Persians. They are roundly insulted...".[24] As a result of harsh and humiliating restrictions and direct forced compulsion, a small part of Mashhadi Jews converted to Islam. The newly-converted Jews in Mashhad as well as in other Iranian towns were named *Djedid ul-Islam* (Arabic for "newly-converted"). In 1839, during one single day, all the other Mashhadi Jews were forcibly converted to Islam by crowds of Shi'ite fanatics. That

---

[15] Conolly, 1834, vol. 2, p. 312.
[16] Ferrier, 1857, p. 121.
[17] Pinkhasi, 1978, p. 13; Netzer, 1985, p. 44.
[18] Khanykov, 1973, p. 133.
[19] Dilmanian, 1997, p. 34; Kupovetskii, 1992, p. 50. Although Kupovetskii names the city Torbat, he, most likely, meant the more economically-developed Torbat-e Haydarieh, instead of Torbat-e Jam.
[20] Wolff, 1837, p. 98.
[21] Fischel, 1936, p. 53
[22] Fraser, 1984, p. 467.
[23] Samuel, 1840, pp. 9-10.
[24] Blaramberg, 1853, p. 235. About the trades plied by Mashhadi Jews he wrote that they, like other Jews, engaged themselves in bargaining and – especially – in turquoise dressing, and Mashhad has a big market in turquoise. Ibid.

day became known as the *Allahdad* (God's Justice). It is described in detail in other works and will not be discussed here.[25] After being converted to Islam, many Djedid Jews of Mashhad like the Chalah (Tajik for "neither one thing nor the other", half-finished, meaning Bukharan Jews who were converted to Sunni Islam)[26] living in adjacent Central Asia, continued to secretly observe the Jewish rituals.[27] By dint of bribes many of them obtained the permission to leave the town, which resulted in the decrease of their population there, by more than two thirds by the middle of the 1840s, according to information of Joseph Ferrier given above. The newly-converted who left town moved to Central Asia (which will be discussed in further detail) and to the following towns: Kabul, Balkh, Tashqurgan and Herat (all in Afghanistan); Yazd, Tehran and Hamadan (all in Iran).[28] Relatively large numbers of Mashhadi

---

[25] Abezguz, 1904, pp. 108-109; Fischel, 1936, pp. 53-54; Gordzhi, 1970, pp. 12-13; Ieshua-Raz, 1992, pp. 105-108; Patai, 1997, pp. 51-63; Wolff, 1846, pp. 332-333. For Mashhadi Jews converting to Islam even in the late 1830s see: Berlin, 1911, p. 154; Moreen, 1986, pp. 217-223; Wolff, 1937, 98, 112; Netzer, 1990, pp. 127-128, 138, 142. Iranian Shah Fath-Ali (1797-1834) had a Jewish wife who had converted to Islam. See: Netzer, 1990, p. 141. In this light, the veracity of the information published in the Jewish paper Voskhod ('Dawn', end of the 19th century) on descendants of Jewesses kidnapped and forced into cohabitation by Moslems, those descendants called in Iran Djedids and disrespected by other Moslems – is doubted. For other information about them see: Evrei v Persii, 1899, p. 1654.
[26] See more details in: Kaganovich, 1997.
[27] Fischel, 1936, pp. 56-63; Ieshua-Raz, 1992, pp. 116-122; Netzer, 1990, p. 144; Wolff, 1846, pp. 332-333.
[28] Fischel, 1936, pp. 63-64, 67; Levene, 1932; Levy, 1980, pp. 71, 72; Naimark, 1889, pp. 63, 66; Pinkhasi, 1978, pp. 14-15; Wolff, 1846, pp. 331-333; Wolff, 1861, vol. 2, p. 48. It is not inconceivable that Jews of Karokh (a town 50 km distant from Herat) who engaged in buying up wool there in the late 1850s (see: Khanykov, 1973, p. 130) were originally from Mashhad.

Jews moved to Dargaz (Darreh Gaz) as well,[29] a settlement in the northern part of Khorasan.

In Afghan towns, Jews of Mashhad openly returned to Judaism because the dominant Islamic doctrine there was that of the Sunnis, and Shi'ites were considered heretics. Herat became the largest center of concentration of Mashhadi Jews outside of their native town. They identified themselves with the local Jewish community, which they outnumbered by far.[30] Consequently, most probably, by the

---

[29] About 70 families of Mashhadi Jews came to Dargaz after their conversion to Islam. Levy, 1987, p. 77; Dilmanian, 1997, p. 37. By the end of the 19th century many of them, assumingly, either migrated to the Russian Transcaspian oblast, or parted with Judaism permanently. The Russian researcher P.M. Vlasov wrote of "an insignificant number of Jews, living there" (i.e. in Dargaz), probably having Djedids in mind. Vlasov, 1894, p. 127. Several waves of expulsion from Turkmenia that took place in the late 1890s, as well as at the beginning of the 20th century, of which later, brought dozens of Mashhadi families, mainly from Marv, to Dargaz – a fact referred to in the memoirs of Farajulla Livian. Patai, 1997, pp. 113-114. The émigrés, who earned their living by intermediate trade between Iran, on the one side, and Bukhara and Turkestanskii krai, on the other side, secretly observed kashrut laws and had two clandestine synagogues. Ibid., pp. 135-137, 142.

[30] As it appears, there were no Jews in Herat at the end of the 18th century. A certain Englishman named Forster, covering his visit to Herat in 1783, said nothing about Jewish residents of the city, even as he wrote of Armenian traders who lived there and compared their commercial methods to those of Jews. Forster, 1798, vol. 2, pp. 115-117. Captain Christie, also an Englishman who visited Herat in 1810, reported of only a few Jews living there (for his report see: Turkestanskie vedomosti, 1884; Sbornik svedeniy, 1885, p. 67). Samuel mentioned Jews among the city inhabitants in 1836, but did not give any information about their number. Samuel, 1840, p. 11. Naimark was told on his travel into Afghanistan in 1886 that in 1840, the year that Mashhadi Jews came over to Herat, there were 20 families of Afghan Jews there. He himself witnessed the presence of 300 Jewish families in Herat. Taking into account the fact that the population of Afghan Jews proper in Herat might have grown in 45 years up to 50 families, we should suppose the number of former Mashhad Jews there to be 250 families at that point. See: Naimark, 1889, p. 66. Speaking of the time the Mashhadi Jews settled down in Herat, one has to bear in mind that it was but the very start of a long-term process of resettling that 1840 saw. The migration on such a scale could hardly be feasible if not scattered over years. Most probably, there was a noticeable increase in the number of Jewish migrants to Herat in the late 1840s, since Ferrier, on his arrival at Herat in 1845, found just a couple of Jewish families there. See: Ferrier, 1857, p. 123. For the Mashhadi origin of most Jews living in Herat, see also: Fischel, 1936, pp. 64-65.

last quarter of the 19th century, originally Herati Jews were assimilated by better educated and wealthier Mashhadi Jews who took the lead of the Jewish community in Herat. With that, because of their new citizenship and place of residence they were called "either Afghani and Herati Djedids or Afghani and Herati Jews" in pre-Revolutionary Russia while other Jews from Mashhad received the name "Mashhadi Djedids". Accordingly, this article will use such names, despite the above-described definition of the term "Djedids," to include not all of the descendants of Mashhadi Jews who converted to Islam, but only those who openly or secretly returned to Judaism, preserving by that their membership in the Jewish community and not assimilating into the Islamic world. The descendants of the newly-converted Mashhadi Jews called themselves Djedids in their official addresses to the Russian authorities instead of calling themselves Jews. The reasons for that will be revealed below. In Mashhad they also were officially called Djedids. And in other Iranian cities they called themselves Moslems from Mashhad in order to hide their Jewish origin.

As for self-identification, until the last quarter of the 19th century the Jews originating in Mashhad called themselves "Mashhadi". In doing so they did not refer to their city of origin, but considered themselves as a separate subethnos within the language and ethnocultural features of the Jewish-Iranian language and ethnoculture (for example, even now, unlike other Jews from Iran, they eat rice dishes on Passover, as they did in the times when they could not use matzoth in Mashhad). From the early 20th century in Eretz-Israel, England and the USA they have their own synagogues separate from other Iranian Jews. Unlike the Mashhadi, the Jewish natives from other Iranian cities, for example, Tehran, Hamadan, Isfahan, Shiraz, Yazd, identify themselves primarily as Persian Jews and only secondarily as natives of the respective cities. Despite strong relations, communications and common language and ethnoculture with other Mashhadi Jews, the Jews from Mashhad who settled in Herat had by the late 19th century assimilated into the old Herat Jewish community and were known as "Heroti". From that time Herati Jews had in fact become a separate subethnic group of the Mashhadi Jews.

Apart from the Jews of Herat, the only significant Jewish community in the territory of modern Afghanistan during the 19th century was in Balkh. Michael Zand considers the Jews of Balkh to be a part of the Bukharan-Jewish ethnos whose dialect they spoke.[31] In other cities of Afghanistan the Jewish population in the 19th century was insignificant and consisted basically of emigrants from Iran and Bukhara. Despite the lack of indigenous Jews at the end of the 19th century, during the 1920's and the 1930's the Jews of Afghanistan were a united political community viewed by Itzhak Bezalel as Afghani Jewry.[32] This was most likely a consequence of Afghanistan's self-isolation during these years. In Eretz-Israel this political association has, over time, led to a change of self-identification by natives of Herat. Those who had not joined the Mashhadi community consider themselves Herati, or Afghani Jews.

Many researchers were interested in the history of Mashhadi Jews in Iran and Afghanistan.[33] However, almost no attention was given to their life in Central Asia except for several articles in Russian.[34] In the meantime, it was Central Asia where Mashhadi Jews achieved considerable improvement in their economic status, and as a consequence, their spiritual level grew as well. It was not by accident that Yakov Dilmanian, the researcher of Mashhadi Jews, laid special emphasis on the "Russian stage" of their history that he sin-

---

[31] Zand, Capture, 1988, p. 56.
[32] Bezalel, 1999, pp. 30-37.
[33] Ben-Zvi, 1966; Fischel, 1936; Ieshua-Raz, 1992; Levy, 1980; Netzer, 1990.
[34] Kaganovich, 1995; Kupovetskii, 1992; Vaisenberg, 1916.

gled out as one of the six periods in their history.³⁵ This paper attempts to fill the vacuum in the history of one of the most interesting Iranian Jewish communities.

Djedid Settlements in Central Asia and Their Population

Some Mashhadi Jews moved to Central Asia in the first third of the 19ᵗʰ century as they escaped religious persecutions. There, they settled in the big towns of the Bukharan Emirate or in the South-East of Turkmenia where they had trading relations with Turkmen tribes, as mentioned before. In the territory of modern Turkmenia where there was no Jewish population by the 19ᵗʰ century³⁶ they had founded their own communities, while in the Emirate of Bukhara, the Kokand Khanate and in the territory of the Turkestanskii krai (a newly formed Russian province governed by a Governor-General in 1867), Djedids returned to Judaism and gradually were assimilated into the Bukharan Jewish circles without forming their own communities. With that, their descendants preserved the story of their ancestry in their family tradition, as, for example, the Abramovs, Babaevs and Pinkhasovs.³⁷

The captain of the East India Company, Alexander Burnes, who visited Bukhara in 1832 and there found Mashhadi Jews, thought that all the four thousand Jews who lived there by then had moved from Mashhad.³⁸ The same view was held by Arminius Vambery, a

---

³⁵ Dilmanian, 1997, p. 11.

³⁶ Kaganovich, Attitude, 2003, pp. 38-39.

³⁷ Fischel, 1936, p. 69; Fischel, 1964, p. 542; Harel, 1983, p. 13; Naimark, 1889, pp. 65, 73; Pinkhasi, 1978, pp. 13-19. Other instances of resettlement and intermingling are given in: Kalontarov, 1963, p. 611; Kupovetskiy, 1992, p. 63; Levy, 1987, p. 77; Wolff, 1861, vol. 2, p. 9. Telling Wolff in 1832 of the Mashhadi Jews who took their residence in Bukhara, rabbi Gadai mentioned a bad reputation they had acquired in the city, on account of their habit of reading books by the Iranian poet Hafiz. Wolff, 1837, p. 126.

³⁸ Burnes, 1839, vol. 2, p. 235.

Hungarian traveler of Jewish origin who visited Central Asia in 1863. According to his records, all Jews had come to Bukhara from Iran and Marv 150 years before.[39] Ephraim Naimark, a Jewish traveler who visited Central Asia in 1886, reported about the Djedids living in Bukhara.[40] None of these travelers provided numbers of their population in Bukhara, nor in other towns of Central Asia. The information about contributions Jews of Bukhara made in 1890 in order to create their quarter in Jerusalem, allows an estimate of their population in the capital town of the Emirate of Bukhara. Thus, 350 people made donations during the year 1890. Among them, 11 (3.14%) had the *lakob* (Arabic for "nickname") "Herati", 2 had the *lakob* "Irani" (0.6%),[41] which suggests their Djedid origin. Most likely, there were other Jews of Djedid origin among the rest of the contributors who had their *lakobs* given not in accordance with their place of origin, but referring to their occupation or by their physical or personal attributes.[42] This seems even more obvious if we take into consideration the fact that it was im-

---

[39] Vambery, 1864, p. 372. Presumably the informants, both of him and of the *Nedelnaia Khronika Voskhoda* correspondent who described the position of the Jews of Bukhara (see: Voskhod, 1889) came from Iran. Olga Sukhareva, in her research of legends about the origin of the Jewish community of Bukhara, has concluded that various versions of the story of how Jews ended up living in Central Asia, represent real stories of multifarious settler families, part of them having reached the region from the territory of Iran, who had amalgamated with time into the Jewish Diaspora of Central Asia. Sukhareva, 1966, pp. 166-167. There was a permanent Jewish population in ancient Marv from at least the beginning of the 4th century until the end of the 15th century. See: Gil, 1997, vol. 1, p. 271, 284, 526; Zand, 1988, pp. 6, 17-18; Fischel, 1945, p. 35-37. The Jewish presence in the town came to an end at a certain point, though. In 1790 the Bukharans destroyed the town, yet the river flowing nearby still continued to be an attraction for Turkmens who made their camps in the vicinity. C.E. Stewart, a British officer, counted as many as 6000 Turkmen tents, as he traveled there in the early 1880s. Stewart, 1977, p. 150. Russians, having annexed Marv oasis in 1884, built a railroad on its territory and founded a town there immediately after, with a railway station as a hub.

[40] Naimark, 1889, p. 65. For Djedids in Bukhara see also: Fischel, 1936, p. 66.

[41] List of denotation, 1890, pp. 1-4.

[42] More information about the origin of Lakobs can be found in: Tolmas, 2001, pp. 87-127.

possible to give everyone the same nicknames. For example, one of the contributors had the *Iakob* "zargar" (jeweler), while it is a well-known fact, that jeweler's art was very popular among Iranian Jews[43] and nothing can be said about other Jews occupied with it until the end of the 19th century. At the same time, our sources have no information about this occupation being popular among Bukharan Jews before that time. Some immigrants from Iran could have been members of *Kohn* and *Levi* casts, which could have been reflected in their name instead of geographically-based nicknames. Therefore, we may suggest that by the end of the 1880s Djedids represented at least 6% of all Bukharan Jews in the town of Bukhara. Taking into account the fact that the Jewish community in the capital town of Bukhara had about 5000 members,[44] the Djedid population in the town may be presumed to be not less than 300 people.

Based on this and taking into account, that Djedids lived in other big towns of Central Asia as well,[45] (excluding Turkmenia, as will be

---

[43] Benjamin, 1859, pp. 211-212; Curzon, 1892, vol. 1, p. 510; Tsadik, 2005, p. 47. About their being engravers see: Samuel, 1840, p. 9. An account of turquoise processing being an occupation of many Iranian Jews can be found in: Blaramberg, 1853, p. 235.

[44] This estimation was issued from the pen of Shmuel Moshe Rivlin, one of the earliest historians of the Bukharan Jews, who lived in the Turkestanskii krai in 1886-1889. Rivlin, 1888, p. 3097. The estimation seems to me to be a perfect truth.

[45] Weissenberg, 1913, p. 260. There are contributors from other places, including those known for their relatively large Jewish population, on the list. On the consideration that those places, in the main, passed to Russia, where Jews used to adopt russified surnames, as derivatives from their father's name, and that it is under those surnames – not under *Iakobs* – they appear on the list, it seems totally impossible to find out the origin of the contributors – even approximately. Nevertheless, the Djedid presence in Samarkand is undoubted, since no less than 3 contributors (2%) appearing on the list have *Iakob* "Herati" instead of their surnames. The official register of Samarkand mentions 6 families of Jewish émigrés from Afghanistan who came over to the city in 1868-1870. TsGHAU, f. 18, op. 1, d. 4468, p. 54. For hundreds of Djedids living in in Samarkand see: Fischel, 1949, p. 32. Though it is known that Iranian Jews had a separate synagogue in the city (Asherov, 1977, p. 24), no traces of a separate Djedid community, either in any town of the Emirate of Bukhara of the Turkestanskii krai, are found in the sources.

THE MASHHADI JEWS (DJEDIDS) IN CENTRAL ASIA   11

discussed below) we may assume that their total population, including the offsprings of Djedid men was 500 people by the end of the 1880s. It was probably the consent of the Emir of Bukhara to the request of the Rabbi of Bukhara, Pinkhas ha-Gadol about the return of Djedids' to Judaism for the Djedids who lived in the territory of Bukhara that contributed to such considerable immigration of Djedids to Central Asia (this request must have dated back to the 1840-1850s).[46] Evidently, the well-known researcher of Iranian Jews, Walter Fischel, was correct when he claimed Djedids to remain faithful to Judaism only owing to the Jews of Central Asia.[47]

In Turkmenia, already in the first third of the 19th century there were communities of Mashhadi Jews. Thus, the above-mentioned Joseph Wolff found 80 families of Mashhadi Jews in the settlement of Serakhs during his first travel around South Turkmenia in 1832, as well as several families of Mashhadi Jews in Annau, Marv and Tejen.[48] Some of those Mashhadi Jews had previously been converted to Islam. In a new place, they openly returned to Judaism and according to Wolff's statement Sunni Turkmens did not put obstacles in their way as they sympathized with them and were not overly fond of Shi'ites.[49] The above-mentioned Burnes, who visited the Serakhs settlement during the same year also stated, that several families of Mashhadi Jews traded with the Turkmenian tribe Salor.[50]

---

[46] Rabin, 1989, pp. 28-29.
[47] Fischel, 1936, p. 73.
[48] Wolff, 1837, pp. 112-113 and after him - Fischel, 1936, p. 53.
[49] Fischel, 1936, p. 53; Wolff, 1837, p. 113; Wolff, 1846, p. 314; Wolff, 1860, pp. 520-521. Turkmens would not do any harm to their Jewish prisoners, while the Shi'ite and Orthodox, to say nothing of pagans, were made slaves when captured by Turkmens. Wolff, 1860, vol. 1, p. 521. Wolff wrote, however, of two Mashhadi Jews who were murdered in Marv and, later on, avenged by a Khiva grandee. Wolff, 1837, p. 124. For Turkmens' tolerance to other religions see also: O'Donovan, 1882, vol. 2, p.130.
[50] Burnes, 1839, vol. 2, pp. 50-51. Though the traveler called the settlement Shurukhs, it is obvious from the itinerary that he meant Serakhs.

The data provided by Wolff must be closer to truth since during his travel, he, unlike Burnes, had contact with Jews in all places. Arminius Vambery who visited Marv in 1863 was surprised by the status of Mashhadi Jews among Turkmenians. Reporting that Mashhadi Jews continued to observe Judaism outside of Mashhad, he wrote, "...The most surprising thing is that Jews here settle even among the most merciless native-Turkmenian predators; a whole Jewish community may even be found in Marv that is always filled with sounds of chain clangs. Living among Turkmenians, however, they themselves turned into half-Turkmenians, but they have their inevitable small payos and head-dress [hat]. Besides, a Turkmenian Jew has his own tent, his own horse, and his own Persian slaves whom he tortures and beats pretty much".[51]

Despite their free status in Turkmenia, some Djedids converted to Sunni Islam out of their own free will. Probably, the majority of such converted Moslems were from among the Djedids who came to Turkmenian territory during the 1840s to 1860s rather than from among those who came later. Wolff must have meant such Jews when he reported during his second travel around Central Asia in 1844 that he met "two Jews from Marv who were converted to Islam and became Turkmenians by their profession and occupation".[52] Some Djedid descendants who converted from Shi'ite Islam to Sunni Islam retained their family stories about their Jewish origin. For example, the well-known poet Pairav (Sulaimoni Atajan, 1899-1933) knew that his grandfather (who was a physician) was a Mashhadi Jew who was converted to Islam in Mashhad and then moved to Marv together with his brothers. All the brothers' offsprings completely left Judaism. During the 1870s-1880s, they moved to Bukhara and traded astrakhan there with Russia and in-

---

[51] Vambery, 1876, p. 254.
[52] Wolff, 1846, pp. 316-317. Information about the permission given to all the Jews who had been converted to Islam back in Iran, to return to their original beliefs and traditions, as soon as they were in Marv, comes from: Wolff, 1861, p. 381.

termarried with Tajiks.[53] Most likely, Dilmanian means his grandfather, when he says hakim Molla Soleiman many years "traded with his brother and business partner Hadji Mohammad Raffi in Mashad, employing Torkaman smugglers." According to this source Soleiman did not want to return to Mashhad and his wife refused to join him in Bukhara. He decided to marry in Bukhara. Since he evidently did not adhere to Jewish ritual. The Jews of Bukhara rejected him as a convert to Islam. He took a Moslem wife and his offspring became Moslems.[54]

During the 1870s-1880s, the status of the Djedids in Herat and other Afghan towns was unstable. In 1870-1871 they suffered hunger and a pogrom. In 1875, during the Uzbek revolt in Maimana, 13 Jews were killed. In 1863 and in 1871, the Iranian Shah Dost Muhammad Khan attacked Herat and robbed the Jews. In 1879, 1881, and in 1885, anti-Jewish pogroms took place in Herat. At the end of 1879, a special tax was imposed upon the Jewish community there, which totaled 2000 tumans. Additionally, the community had to send 300 people to fortify the town walls. In 1877, a special decree was issued in Afghanistan recruiting Jews for the army, and about 2000 Jews escaped the country.[55]

In Mashhad and in other places of Khorasan, Djedids often suffered from outbreaks of famine that took place in Iran. They happened during the following years: 1860-1861, 1879-1880, but the most terrible one was the famine of 1869-1872 when about 10% of the Iranian population died.[56] As the Vilna newspaper in Hebrew

---

[53] Suleimani, 1966, p. 530. Apparently, their families sympathized to Jews. For example, Pairav himself wrote plays for the Samarkand theater of Bukharan Jews during the Soviet period. Zand, 1977, p. 162.
[54] Dilmanian, 1997, p. 34.
[55] Jews in Afghanistan, 1878; Iz Herata, 1880; Gordzhi, 1970, pp. 144-159; Mishal, 1981, p. 209.
[56] Ivanov, 1952, p. 193.

Ha-Karmel reported, during that famine there was no one there to bury the dead.[57]

Djedids from Iranian and Afghan towns felt safer in Central Asia in general and in Turkmenia in particular,[58] which resulted in continuous migration to that region during the second half of the 19th century. According to the Russian administration, of the Mashhadi Djedids who lived in Marv at the beginning of the 20th century, three families moved there during the 1860s and nine families during the 1870s.[59] According to the same source, 14 families of Afghan Djedids moved to Marv during the 1870s.[60] These data confirm the information of the Russian officer Mahksud Alikhanov-Avarskiy, an Avar and a son of a close associate of Imam Shamil. According to his data, 26 Jewish families lived in Marv at the beginning of the 1880s.[61] According to another Russian administrative source, four Afghan and forty Iranian Djedid families moved to Marv during the 1870s.[62] These data seem to be more reliable than the information of the reporter of the London *Daily News*, Edmund O'Donovan, an Irishman, stating that there were only seven Jewish families in Marv in 1880.[63] Additionally, his report is supported by the data provided by P.M. Lessar,[64] a Russian

---

[57] The Famine in Persia, 1872.
[58] Absence of full statistical data on Djedids living in Iranian and Afghan towns does not allow one to evaluate the decrease in population of those communities. Data on Herat shows a decrease in the number of Jewish families there, from 300 (see above) to 250 (see: Letters from Jerusalem, 1896), in 1885-1896.
[59] Central Historical State Archive of Uzbekistan, Tashkent (hereafter: TsGHAU), f. 1, op. 17, d. 922, pp. 113-118a.
[60] Ibid, p. 109.
[61] Alikhanov, 1883, p. 32. Landsell seemingly drew information from the same source. Lansdell, 1885, vol. 2, p. 477.
[62] TsGHAU, f. 1, op. 17, d. 848, pp. 61a., 78-79.
[63] O'Donovan, 1882, vol. 2, p. 129. It was presumably the fear of punishment they might have incurred for their return to Judaism if they would visit Iran that made them hide the fact that they had come from Mashhad. For details of Edmond O'-Donovan's visit to Turkmenia see: Khalfin, 1965, pp. 356-357.
[64] Lessar, 1884, p.195; O'Donovan, 1882, vol. 2, p. 378.

political agent in Bukhara, an administrative official who oversaw the vassal Emirate government. Apparently, they had their own small settlement near Koushut Kala (not far from Serakhs) at the border with Iran (along with Djedids, only a few Kazakh families lived there). By the year 1886, the number of Djedids living in Serakhs had decreased, probably as a result of their migration to Koushut Kala, Tejen and Marv. In 1886, only 10 Djedid families[65] lived there as compared to the 80 families, mentioned above. According to the information of the Russian administration, by the time that the Marv oasis was conquered in 1884, 58 Djedid families lived there[66] including 15 Afghan Djedids living in Marv.[67] All other Djedids must therefore have come from Mashhad. During the second half of the 1880s, another five Djedid families moved to Marv from Herat.[68] The foregoing data of the Russian administration about the Djedid population in Marv is corroborated by the data of the above-mentioned Naimark, according to which 80 families lived there in 1886 (60 families from Mashhad and 20 from Herat).[69] According to the report of G. Dobson, by the end of the 1880s, 249 Jews lived in Marv, evidently including about two hundred Djedids.[70] Among the 18 independent Iranian Djedids who, according to administrative information, moved to Tejen[71] during 1885-1889, the majority were obviously Mashhadi Djedids who came from Serakhs.

According to the data of the clerk of the Russian Ministry of Foreign Affairs, P.M. Lessar, in 1884 few Djedids lived in the territory

---

[65] Naimark, 1889, p. 67.
[66] TsGHAU, f. 1, op. 17, d. 922, p. 92.
[67] Ibid, p. 109; Leivi, 1930, p.18.
[68] TsGHAU, f.1, op.17, d. 922, p. 109.
[69] Naimark, 1889, p. 68.
[70] Dobson, 1890, p. 319. Along with Djedids, as many as fifty Bukharan Jews lived in Marv at the time. D. Leivi wrote of 25 Bukharan Jews living in Marv in 1884; in 1898 there were 108 of them in the Transcaspian oblast. Leivi, 1930, p. 18.
[71] TsGHAU, f. 1, op. 17, d. 922, pp. 88-88a.

that belonged to the tribe of Saryks (including the settlements: Iolatan, Pende and Kushka). Lessar called them "Jews from Herat". He also reported, that they sent their children to Herat to study in a *medreseh*.[72] He must have been referring to a Jewish school. Family lists, dated back to the beginning of the 20th century, give information about the Djedid population in Pende *pristavstvo* (a small administrative unit), probably in the very settlement of Pende. According to these lists, by the end of the 1870s, 25 Herat Djedids and one Mashhad Djedid lived there.[73] During the second half of the 1880s five more Afghan Djedids settled there.[74] According to Naimark, in 1886 20 Djedids lived in Iolatan who engaged in peddling and who, just like the Marv Djedids, had left their families both in Mashhad and Herat.[75]

According to the Russian administration, by 1881 when Russians conquered it[76], 23 Djedid families lived in the Akhal-Tekin oasis, mostly in its center Kizyl-Arvat. Only one Djedid lived in the Turkmen settlement Otamysh who settled there in the middle of the 1870s.[77] Only one Mashhadi Djedid family lived in Takhta-Bazar by the time it was conquered by the Russians in 1884.[78]

Thus, taking into account that many Djedids left their families in Iran or Afghanistan, we may assume that by the middle of the 1880s about five hundred Djedids lived in the territory of the Transcaspian oblast that was formed in the conquered Turkmenian lands (this oblast was part of the Caucasus vicegerency till 1899 and then of the Turkestanskii krai[79]). This number included: 120 Dje-

---

[72] Lessar, Turkmenistan, 1884, p. 20.
[73] TsGHAU, f. 1, op. 17, d. 922, p. 110-110a.
[74] Ibid.
[75] Naimark, 1889, pp. 68-69.
[76] TsGHAU, f. 1, op. 17, d. 922, p. 92.
[77] Ibid, p. 158.
[78] TsGHAU, f. 1, op. 17, d. 848, p. 86.
[79] By the end of the 19th century, the territory of the Governor-Generalship included the oblasts of Syrdaria, Samarkand, Ferghana, Semirechye and Transcaspi-

dids living in Marv, 100 in Kizyl-Arvat, 100 in Koushut Kala, 50 in Serakhs, 50 in Tejen, 26 in Pende, 20 in Iolatan, 5 in Chaacha, 5 in Takhta-Bazar. As mentioned above, approximately the same number of Djedids who left Afghanistan and Iran between 1840 and 1885, lived in other Central Asia administrative regions – in the Khanate of Khiva, in Bukhara and in the Turkestanskii krai, which was formed in 1867. Thus, about a thousand Djedids lived in Central Asia by the middle of the 1880s. However, many Djedids of Bukhara and the Turkestanskii krai, as was stated above, became part of the Jewish ethnic community in Bukhara.

Djedids were not the only migrants from Iran to Russia. Difficult economic and unstable political conditions led to a constant increase of the number of Iranians among the migrants coming to Russia. While during the 1870s, 11.7% of all immigrants were Iranians, during the 1880s it became 8.5%, and during the 1890s they reached 43%![80] During this time, the number of Iranian immigrants to Russia increased in absolute numbers as well. While in 1876, 13 thousand Iranians entered Russia crossing the Southern border, in 1900, 67.3 thousand people migrated and in 1913, 274.5 thousand people came to Russia. Year by year, the number of Iranians staying in Russia increased as well. While in 1900, the difference between Iranians entering and leaving Russia was 9.8 thousand, in 1913 it increased to a total of 61.2 thousand.[81]

Some evidence of Djedid population in the Transcaspian oblast at the end of the 19th century is available. According to the data provided by the English traveler and Judaica collector, E.N. Adler, who visited Marv in 1897, 50-60 Djedid families lived there at the

---

an. All of them were divided on *uyezds* and *uyezds* were divided into *volosts*, *volosts* - into *pristavstvos*. The Governor-General's residence was in the principal town of the Syrdaria oblast, Tashkent.

[80] Kabuzan, 1998, pp. 152-153.

[81] Entner, 1965, p. 60. I thank Azaria Levy for showing me this source.

time.[82] Some of them concealed their devotion to Judaism, while others observed Jewish traditions openly by calling themselves Djedid Jews.[83] Adler's statement, that Russian administration encouraged Jewish immigration from Mashhad[84] is incorrect, as will be shown below. According to the data of D. Leivi, by the year 1899, 255 Mashhadi and, mainly, Herat Djedids lived in the whole Transcaspian oblast.[85] He must have meant only grown-up men. The data of the All-Russian population census conducted in the Transcaspian oblast in 1897 are greatly understated and inaccurate,[86] therefore it cannot be a reliable source even regarding the Jewish population of the oblast.

Relatively accurate figures on the Djedid population in the Transcaspian oblast in the very beginning of the 20th century may be found in the data of the Russian administration.

Table 1. Djedid population in the Transcaspian oblast in 1902 according to their citizenship[87]

Place	Citizens of Iran	Citizens of Afghanistan	Total

---

[82] Adler, Jews in Many Lands, 1905, p. 214.
[83] Budushchnost', 1902.
[84] Adler, Jews in Many Lands, 1905, pp. 214-215.
[85] Leivi, 1930, p. 18.
[86] Bekmakhanova, 1986, p. 252.
[87] TsGHAU, f. 1, op. 17, d. 922, pp. 88-88a., 105-118a. The data on Ashgabat are only an approximate evaluation. Fischel stated that less than fifty Djedid families were living there at the beginning of the 20th century. See: Fischel, 1936, p. 66. Most likely, though, those were adult males, not families, he had in mind, the number of Djedids being otherwise too large to remain unheeded by the local authorities and unmentioned in the official documents. Taking into account that the number of females and minors was insignificant, as we see in the table, and also the fact that Adler wrote of just a couple of Djedid families taking residence in Ashgabat (Adler, 1905, p. 214), it is most probable that there were no more than 70 Djedid inhabitants in the city at that time. Active measures the Russians took to evict Djedids from Ashgabat are mentioned in: Abezgauz, 1904, p. 109.

	Adult men[88]	all	Adult men	all	Adult men	all
Marv	92	158[89]	39	94	131	252
Pende	17	22	76	76	93	98
Bairam-Ali	-	-	3	3	3	3
Iolatan	-	-	23	27	23	27
Tejen uezd[90]	49	49	3	3	52	52
Ashgabat	?	?	?	?	50	70
Total, Transcaspian oblast	158	229	144	203	352	502

Thus, the number of Djedids in Turkmenia during the previous 17 years of Russian rule remained almost unchanged. This was due to a policy that included both eviction and entry restriction. This policy, which will be discussed below, was applied during the second half of the 1890s. At the same time, the statistics of the Djedid population were, to a certain extent, affected by the cholera epidemic of 1892-1893, that spread in many regions of Central Asia and in Afghanistan as well.[91]

According to our estimate, a quarter of the two thousand Jews living in Mashhad at the end of the 1830s left Judaism within the next forty years. Therefore, by 1885, the Djedid population had grown to 3,350 people, taking into account an annual estimated natural increase of 1.8%. However, by that time, as was shown above, about 500 of them joined the communities of the Bukharan Jews, and the

---

[88] I.e. self-dependent males of at least 13 years of age.

[89] Besides these Mashhadi Djedids 9 Jews from Teheran lived in Marv. TsGHAU, f. 1, op. 17, d. 922, p. 109.

[90] In the Tejen uezd Djedids lived in Tejen, Serakhs, Koushut Kala and Chaacha.

[91] The item about numerous victims among Jews of Marv is from: Gordzhi, 1970, pp. 151, 156-157. For that epidemic in the total of Central Asia see: Aini, 1960, p. 451; Kaganovich, Attitude, 2003, p. 96. Details about that epidemic in Herat and information on Jewish victims can be found in: Gordzhi, 1970, pp. 150-151.

sub-ethnic community of Djedids including its Herati branch counted about 2,850 members. Estimating the annual natural increase to be the same as above, by 1902 this population had to be 3,860 people. Then, taking into account the data given in Table 1, the number of Djedids living in the Transcaspian oblast was 13%. At the same time, as can be seen in the table, many Djedids lived in the Transcaspian oblast separated from their families.[92] Every adult Djedid in average had left behind 4 dependent family members in Herat, Mashhad and other Afghan and Iranian towns. This totals more than a thousand family members.

Due to natural increase and a certain liberalization of the Russian administration in its approach to the Djedids between 1900 and 1910, their population in the Transcaspian oblast tripled between the years 1902 and 1910 to more than 1,500 people. This phenomenon will be described below in further detail.

Table 2. *Djedid population in the Transcaspian oblast in 1910 according to their citizenship*[93]

Place	Citizens of Iran		Citizens of Afghanistan		Total	
	Adult men[94]	All	Adult men	All	Adult men	All
Marv	202	356[95]	47	*147*	249	*503*[96]
Pende	28	73[97]	107	*267*	135	*340*

[92] About that see also: Pilosof-Pinkhasof, 1970, p. 23.
[93] TsGHAU, f. 1, op. 17, d. 848, pp. 60a., 66, 74-94; Ibid, d. 922, p. 8. Evaluation data on the total Djedid population in some localities are printed in italics. They are arrived at by multiplying the total number of adult males in those places by the family size index of each particular place found based upon the statistics.
[94] I.e., self-dependent males of at least 13 years of age.
[95] 25 adult men had their families in Iran.
[96] These data differs from the estimation N. Slousch, according to whom in Marv uezd in 1909 lived 60 Iranian Djedid families and 20 Herati Jews families among whom, apparently, also were Djedids. Slousch, 1909, p. 412.

Takhta-Bazar	47	77[98]	-	-	47	77
Bairam-Ali	18	26[99]	9	1 0[100]	27	36
Atek pristavstvo	25	95	-	-	25	95
Serakhs	40	181	-	-	40	181
Iolatan	-	-	69	*75*	69	*75*
Tejen uezd[101]	?	210	-	-	?	210
Total, Transcaspian oblast	360	1018	232	*499*	592	*1517*

The number of Djedids, who were Iranian citizens increased by 4.5 times. Given this fact, the number of those Djedids with Iranian citizenship among all the Djedids of the oblast increased during this period of time from one half to two thirds (from 53% to 67.1%).[102] This was a result of a less tolerant attitude towards the Afghan Djedids, apparently on account of their Afghan citizenship. Unlike Iran, where Russian influence was quite high at that time, Afghanistan was controlled by England. English activities, again, aroused the suspicion of the Russians in the region.

By 1910 the number of Djedids of the Transcaspian oblast was 34% of all the Djedids in general, whose population must have been 4,450 people, taking the above noted coefficient into consideration. This number is close to the estimated Djedid population in Iran, Afghanistan and Central Asia constituting 850 families. This is according to data provided by Aba Lev[103] who gathered informa-

---

[97] 6-7 adult men had their families in Iran.
[98] 4 adult men had their families in Iran and 2 - in Samarkand.
[99] 4 adult men had their families in Iran and 3 - in Marv.
[100] 2 adult men had their families in Afghanistan and 4 - in Marv.
[101] Doesn't include Serakhs and Atek pristavstvo.
[102] The number does not include the number of Djedids living in Ashgabat in 1902, no relevant data being provided.
[103] Lev, 1913, c. 3.

tion about the Djedids at that time. As we can see in Table 2, the number of adult men (592) was especially high among the Djedids of the Transcaspian oblast. A Mashhadi Jew stated in 1925, that most of the Djedids moved from Mashhad to Russia for reasons of trade.[104] This is understood to mean adult men, who moved to the region at the beginning of the 1900s. Assuming, that all 4,450 Djedids constituted about 900 families (5 people per family), and the fact that a number of itinerant Djedids at that time were occupied in their business undertakings in other oblasts of the Turkestanskii krai with their families living in Iran or Afghanistan, the statement made above must be true with respect to adult men. In this connection statement of Yaghoub Dilmanian, that during this period two thirds of all Mashhadi Jews lived in Turkmenia seems a little bit overestimated.[105] But we must take into consideration, that many Djedids lived in the Transcaspian oblast temporarily because the Russian administration prohibited their permanent settlement together with their families in the oblast, as will be shown below.

During the first decade of the 20th century, Djedids were threatened with eviction. During 1911-1912, the administration actively evicted about 1,400 Djedids beyond the boundaries of the Russian Empire. As a result of this eviction, only 101 Djedids remained in the Marv uezd: 70 Djedids lived in Marv, 30 in Iolatan, 1 in Takhta-Bazar; and 12 Djedids remained in the Tejen uezd including 2 in Tejen, 7 in Chaacha and 1 in Serakhs.[106] Thus, in the whole Transcaspian oblast, only 113 Djedids were able to prove to the Russian administration that their ancestors had settled in those places before 1880.

---

[104] Fischel, 1936, p. 65. This confirms the Fischel's remark about Djedids who "have mastered the Russian language and Russianized their surnames". Ibid. Russian official registers prove that those of Mashhadi and Herati Jews who used to stay in the Russian territory on a regular basis Russianized their names. As for the Russianization of Djedid names, see, for example: TsGHAU, f. 1, op. 17, d. 922, pp. 105-118a.
[105] Dilmanian, 1997, p. 53.
[106] Obzor, 1913, p. 101.

Further evictions led to a further decrease of the Djedid population in the oblast. Thus, according to administrative data, 76 Djedids lived in the Marv uezd in 1914, 68 of them living in Marv, 7 in Iolatan, 1 in Takhta-Bazar; and 14 Djedids lived in the Tejen uezd including 7 in Tejen, 6 in Serakhs and 1 in Chaacha.[107]

Immediately after the February Revolution of 1917, that abolished religious restrictions in Russia, many Djedids returned to the Transcaspian oblast (Turkmen Soviet Republic from 1924 on) and to other oblasts of the Turkestanskii krai (mainly Uzbek Soviet Republic from 1924 on) as well. After the Bolshevik Revolution in October of the same year, many Djedids continued to come to Turkmenia due to commercial interest. During those years, many Djedids moved their families to the Soviet Central Asian region as well.[108] An especially large number of Mashhadi and Herati Jews settled again in South-Eastern Turkmenia, the large part of which, including the towns of Bairam-Ali, Iolatan, Chaacha, Kushka, Marv, Pende, Serakhs, Takhta-Bazar, and Tejen, formed a part of the Marv uezd. In 1918, when Marv was finally taken under the Bolshevik rule which imposed significant taxes on Mashhadi and Herati

---

[107] Prilozhenie, 1916, attachments VI and VII. This information disagrees to a point with the account published by S.E. Vaisenberg, one of the earliest experts in the anthropology and ethnography of Jews in Russia, who visited the Turkestanskii krai in 1912. According to his account, 200 Djedid families were living in Marv at the time. However, he wrote in the same work that even before the eviction, the Djedid population of the town numbered no more than 100 families. The number of Djedids living in Marv seems to be overestimated by Idelzon as well; this author wrote of 50 Bukharan Jews (i.e. Djedids, as it can be understood by his own mentioning of the eviction that befell other local Jews) in Marv, 50 – in Iolan (Iolatan), and 100 – in Takhta-Bazar. Idelzon, 1920, p. 10. Conversely, he probably underestimated the number of the Jewish residents of Herat, stating there were only 200 of them in the city. Figures provided by Idelzon are definitely incorrect. Thus, his estimation of the number of Bukharan Jews living in Bukhara stretched as far as 15,000, which strikingly disagrees with our estimation: 2,500 people in 1914.

[108] Comes from an interview with a Herati Jew Me'ir Mekhtiyev, taken in Israel on October 25, 2003 (from the author's own archive). Livian mentioned his leaving Dargaz for Marv after February 1917 in his memoirs. Patai, 1997, p. 137. In the same 1917, the family of Suleiman Yudakov came to live in Marv from Iran, presumably from Khorasan. Dakhtaev, 1992, p. 122.

Jews, about 160 families escaped to Khorasan[109] and to the Afghan towns Maimana, Anhoy, Shibarkan, Balkh and Mazari-Sherif.[110] Among the Djedids, who returned to Afghan territory, there was Mishael Ben Avram Agayev Bakhshi. While his family lived in Herat, he started trading in the town of Shibarkan where Turkmens lived.[111] After the USSR changed its economic policy in 1921 (will be discussed below), several men and even whole Djedid families again moved to Turkmenia.

According to the census of 1926, that included only Soviet citizens by their ethnos, 532 Jews lived in the Marv okrug (district, the term uezd changed to okrug in 1924) including one Georgian Jew, 60 Central Asian Jews (this was the official name of Bukharan Jews) and 471 other Jews[112] that obviously included mainly Mashhadi and Herati Jews and Ashkenazi Jews (there were only five or six families of Ashkenazi Jews in Marv itself).[113] The data provided by the same census about the native language, that included foreign citizens as well, show that 904 people living in the Marv okrug stated their native language to be Jewish.[114] All Jewish ethnic groups living there may have considered their dialect to be Jewish. Subtracting 532 Soviet citizens from 904 Jews, we receive 372 Jews having foreign citizenship. Obviously, they all were Djedids. Thus, 820 Mashhadi and Herati Jews were registered by this census either by Jewish ethnos or by Jewish language. Besides, a certain part of Djedids might have stated their native language to be Persian, not excluding their dialect as an independent Jewish language. Some of the Djedids, taught by

---

[109] Mishal, 1981, p. 23; Patai, 1997, p. 139. According to Raphael Patai, Marv Djedids had to pay a half of the tax that was imposed on the merchants. Ibid., p. 137. It could hardly be called a just, equally shared taxation in case of Djedids, since the commerce of the trade conducted by the local Djedids at that time must have been less than a half of the total trade commerce of Marv.

[110] Mishal, 1981, p. 23.

[111] Ibid.

[112] Census, 1926, table VI, p. 13.

[113] TsGARU, f. 86, op. 1, d. 3659, p. 102.

[114] Census, 1926, table VIII, p. 28.

their previous bitter experience, may have concealed their Jewishness out of fear of anti-Semitic actions by the government. Therefore, we might assume that the real number of Mashhadi and Herati Jews living in the territory of the Marv okrug was not less than a thousand: 450 Soviet citizens and 550 foreign – Afghan and Iranian – citizens. These numbers correspond with the information of the Russian demographer Mark Kupovetskii, that by the middle of the 1920s, Mashhadi and Herati Jews living in the settlements of the Marv okrug (Marv, Iolatan, and Takhta-Bazar) formed their separate communities.[115]

The total number of Iranian and Afghan Jews living in the Turkmen Soviet Republic in 1926 was two thousand, according to the data of Aronson, the secretary of a committee for national minority matters under the Central Executive Committee of the Uzbek Soviet Republic.[116]

By our estimate, another 300 Mashhadi and Herati Jews, mostly Afghan and Iranian citizens, lived in other republics of Soviet Central Asia at that time, primarily in the towns of Samarkand, Bukhara and Tashkent. They came to Russia after the beginning of the 20th century and, therefore, were not yet assimilated by Bukharan Jews. Thus, 2,300 Mashhadi and Herati Jews lived in the territory of Soviet Central Asia in 1926, i.e. 39% of the total Djedid population that, taking into consideration the above-given coefficient of natural increase, must have been 5,900 people. This estimate is very different from the apparently overstated estimate of the Russophone Jewish newspaper published in Paris, *Evreiskaia Tribuna*, which reported in 1922 that the number of all Djedids in the world was ten thousand people.[117]

Most probably, half of the Djedid population of Central Asia illegally escaped over the border to Iran and Afghanistan in conse-

---
[115] Kupovetskii, 1992, pp. 59-60.
[116] TsGARU, f. 86, op. 1, d. 3659, p. 104.
[117] Evreiskaia tribuna, 1922.

quence of the policy of economic and religious "strangulation" during the late 1920s and early the 1930s.[118] A certain part of Djedids made their way to Palestine and England.[119]

According to the estimate of Samad ben Joseph Dalmani that was made in 1945, the total number of Djedids in the world in the 1930s was 4,650 people. However, making his calculations, he presumed that only fifty Djedids lived in Southern Turkmenia, mainly in Serakhs.[120]

Meanwhile, the real number of Djedids in Southern Turkmenia and in all Central Asia was much higher. In many towns and villages, they joined the communities of Bukharan Jews. According to the estimate received by M. Kupovetskii about Mashhadi and Herati Jews of South-Eastern Turkmenia, apparently more than a thousand Herati and Mashhadi Jews remained in the USSR by the middle of the 1930s.[121] A complaint of Ashkenazi Jews of the town of Novaia Bukhara (renamed to Kagan in 1935) testifies, that Herati and Mashhadi Jews lived in other places of Central Asia as well. The complaint was lodged with the central administration of the Uzbek authorities, who closed the synagogue where Afghan and Iranian citizens attended as well.[122]

According to the published materials of the population census of 1937, 164 Jews having Afghan citizenship lived in the USSR, which should have meant mainly Djedids from Herat. Although the number of Afghan citizens was the third largest one among alien Jews registered in the USSR, the compilers did not indicate exactly in which Soviet republics they lived, as they did concerning the citizens of ten other countries.[123] Taking into account the places of

---

[118] Fischel, 1936, pp. 67, 73; Kupovetskii, 1992, p. 60. Ben-Zion Ieshua-Raz wrote of 2,000 runaways. Ieshua-Raz, 1992, p. 133.
[119] Fischel, 1936, pp. 70-72.
[120] Ieshua-Raz, 1992, p. 131.
[121] Kupovetskii, 1992, p. 60.
[122] State Archive of Russian Federation, Moscow, f. 5263, op. 1, d. 88, p. 5.
[123] Motrevich and Proshchenok, 1997, pp. 30-33.

their traditional settlement, information from the table on general number of foreign citizens in different republics of the USSR and the fact that alien Ashkenazi Jews lived mostly in the territory of the European part of the country, we may assume that 123 Afghan Djedids lived in Turkmenia, 28 in Uzbekistan, and 13 in Tajikistan. According to the same materials, Iranian Jews were the largest group of alien Jews living in the USSR. The majority of them lived in Georgia and in Azerbaijan, and therefore we may agree with the authors that in the main these were the so-called Kurdish Jews, the Lakhlukhs. As for the mentioned republics of Central Asia, we suppose that the matter concerns Mashhadi Jews, whose population was 63 people including 22 in Turkmenia, 36 in Uzbekistan, and 5 in Tajikistan.[124] Thus, this population census registered 227 Mashhadi and Herati Jews having foreign citizenship. Taking into account that some of the questioned had reasons, quite well-founded as will be shown further, to conceal their Jewishness (they could have said they were Muslims, which was customary), we may assume that the real number of Mashhadi and Herati Jews among foreign citizens was larger by several hundreds. Apparently, alien Djedids formed about half of this sub-ethnic group. Most likely, they kept their foreign citizenship in the hope of leaving the USSR.

Starting with summer of 1937 and until winter of 1938, the Soviet authorities issued a series of resolutions regarding "bourgeois nationalists, agents of foreign special services". This resulted, on the one hand, in numerous arrests of ethnic people who did not have their own republics in the USSR – up to 21.6% of all arrested on political matters in 1937-1939 (71.4% of them were shot immediately after they were arrested);[125] and on the other hand, in ethnic evictions, during which, for example, 170 thousand Koreans who lived in the Soviet Far East and about two thousand Kurds who

---

[124] Ibid.
[125] The calculation is based on: Kostyrchenko, 2001, p. 132.

lived in Caucasus were moved in 1937 to Kazakhstan, Kyrgyzstan and Uzbekistan.[126]

During this campaign, a "purge" of the Southern borders from "unreliable elements" took place, which made the community of Mary (Marv was renamed to oblast center Mary in 1937) suffer especially great losses. In 1938, according to the data of M. Kupovetskii that he received from his informants, almost all adult men of this community who kept their Iranian or Afghan citizenship were arrested and accused of "disruption of the state's security". Some of them were sentenced to long terms of imprisonment in camps, and some were shot in Mary. As we can evaluate, this led to a reduction of the population of Mashhadi and Herati Jews in the USSR by 15-20%.[127] During the same years or several years earlier, Djedids were evicted from the near-border settlements Kerki, Takhta-Bazar and Serakhs to Bairam-Ali and Iolatan which were situated a little more to the north from the border.[128]

Such measures were undertaken in Central Asia not only against alien Jews, but against Moslems as well. Thus, according to Faridun Yusupov, all Moslems having Iranian citizenship were arrested during the same year in Kyrgyzstan. Their destiny was the same.[129]

According to the census of 1939, 582 Jews having Soviet citizenship lived in Mary oblast (term *okrug* was changed to oblast in 1939).[130] The census did not single out separate sub-ethnical Jewish groups, but taking into account that this territory was traditionally the main place of residence of Mashhadi and Herati Jews, we may

---

[126] Polian, 2001, pp. 91-94.

[127] Kupovetskii, 1992, p. 60. Among the arrested Jews was Mekhtiyev's father, an Afghan citizen. Interview with Me'ir Mekhtiyev, October 25, 2003 (from the author's own archive).

[128] According to Population of Russia, 2000, p. 334 and the information received by Kupovetskii, 1992, p. 60 the eviction of Djedids was put into action in 1937-1938. But Mekhtiyev believes it to have occurred in 1934-1935. Interview with Me'ir Mekhtiyev, October 25, 2003 (from the author's own archive).

[129] Yusupov, 1993, p. 88.

[130] Census, 1939, p. 12.

assume that they constituted about a half of all registered Jews, which was about 300 people. Besides, probably several hundred family members of arrested Mashhadi and Herati Jews having foreign citizenship lived in Mary oblast but were not included in the population census. About half a thousand from this sub-ethnic group probably lived in other oblasts of Turkmenistan and in other republics of the USSR.

During the 1950-1960s, the population of this ethnic group in the USSR increased through its birth rate, but during the 1970s it decreased again as a consequence of the fact that several dozens of families emigrated to Israel.[131]

According to the estimate by M. Kupovetskii, by the end of the 1980s their population in the territory of the USSR was not higher than a thousand. In Mary oblast, Mashhadi and Herati Jews lived in Iolatan (about 160), in Bairam-Ali (130) and in Mary (several dozens). Several families lived also in other towns of Turkmenia: in Ashgabat, Charjui, and Kerki. Besides, several hundreds of Mashhadi and Herati Jews lived in Uzbekistan and in Tajikistan, mainly in the towns of Samarkand, Dushanbe, and Tashkent. At the same time, in Iolatan, 10% of Mashhadi and Herati Jews were married to Bukharan Jews, in Bairam-Ali – more than 20%, in Mary – about a third, and in Samarkand, Dushanbe and Tashkent, such marriages were the overwhelming majority.[132]

In the 1990s, almost all Mashhadi and Herati Jews left Turkmenia and, obviously, other Central Asian republics, for Israel, the USA and Germany.[133]

---

[131] Kupovetskii, 1992, p. 60.
[132] Ibid, pp. 60-61.
[133] Interview with Me'ir Mekhtiyev, October 25, 2003 (from the author's own archive).

Legal Status in the Transcaspian oblast until Year 1917

The Djedid population in Turkmenia depended directly on the attitude of the administration towards them. The Turkmenian tribal elite took to them kindly and patronized them. The attitude of a new Russian administration towards Djedids, although variable depending on the oblast chief's personal stance, tended to worsen gradually, which was a reflection of the attitude towards Jews of the central authorities of Russian Empire in general. Even Djedids who settled in the territory of Turkmenia before it was conquered in the early 1880s were viewed by the Russian administration as foreign Jews unwanted in Russia. And this in spite of the fact that before Turkmenia was conquered, Djedids helped Russian Kazaks to arrange their escapes from Turkmenian captivity[134] and were supporters of Russians since they were connected with Russia by commercial interest, as will be shown further. Such attitude was different from the attitude towards Bukharan Jews who lived in the territory of Central Asia, conquered by Russia during the 1860-1870s. They received Russian citizenship and a status of "natives" that almost equalized them in rights not only with local Moslems but also with the Russian Orthodox population.[135] Despite the fact that in 1872 an amendment to act was issued that allowed granting Russian citizenship to Jews having citizenship of Asian countries adjacent to Turkestanskii krai, the local authorities did not spread it to the Transcaspian oblast. Only one Djedid, Moshe Abramov, of whom we will write further, was granted Russian citizenship for his services.[136] The difference between attitudes towards Djedids and towards Bukharan Jews was over the fact that during the early 1880s, the period of conservatism changed the period of reforms in Rus-

---

[134] Von der Hoffen, 1900, no. 26, p. 530.
[135] Kaganovich, Attitude, 2003, pp. 45-46.
[136] TsGHAU, f. 1, op. 17, d. 936, p. 333. For this amendment see: Kaganovich, Attitude, 2003, p. 47.

sia, which was a result of, on the one hand, the murder of the reformer Tsar Alexander II by members of the revolutionary organization "Narodnaia Volia", and on the other hand, with fear of various strata of Russian society from accelerated modernization. After the Russians conquered Marv oasis and widened the Transcaspian oblast, more Djedids moved there from Afghanistan and Khorasan. Probably, like Chalah Jews (Bukharan Jews converted to Islam and secretly observing Judaism) who escaped from the Emirate of Bukhara to the Turkestanskii krai between the end of the 1860s and the 1890s,[137] they thought that they would feel safer under Russian rule and would be able to openly return to Judaism. Although the chief of the Transcaspian oblast in 1883-1890, Military governor A.V. Komarov, the conqueror of Marv oasis, evicted Ashkenazi Jews, he did not prohibit Afghan, Mountain or Bukharan Jews from settling in the oblast.[138] The same may be said about Mashhadi Jews. Under his government, Djedids started moving from Serakhs and other small settlements of Turkmenia to economic and administrative centers of the oblast – Marv and Tejen. Probably, Komarov wanted to widen trade with Iran and Afghanistan through Mashhadi and Herati Jews, since during the same time Russia endeavored to develop trading relations with those countries.[139] During the same period, the head of Marv uezd M. Alikhanov-Avarsky who despaired to increase the population of the uezd center on the account of Turkmens living around in their tents, started to invite Djedids who lived side by side with Turkmens to settle in Marv as well. They didn't agree until Alikhanov, who aimed at developing the newly-created town, delivered them an ultimatum: either they leave the uezd or start building their

---

[137] Kaganovich, 1997, pp. 68-71.
[138] Rivlin, 1887.
[139] Ataev, 1971, p. 14.

houses and shops.[140] Upon that, Djedids started to actively build and buy houses, which we will further discuss.

The new Military governor of the Transcaspian oblast A.N. Kuropatkin (in office in 1890-1899), from the first days of his government, strived to evict Ashkenazi and Mountain Jews.[141] In 1895 Kuropatkin began to abridge the residence right of Jews who were citizens of Afghanistan, Iran and Bukhara as well. The Russian administration refused to extend visas to many of them for their further residence in the Russian Empire. As an exception, an eviction of Jews who traded with Afghanistan was delayed with a view to help Russian merchants open trading relations with that country. However, Kuropatkin ordered uezd superiors to thoroughly register them and thoroughly keep a wary eye on their activity in order not to allow usury and espionage.[142]

The Russian administration most likely feared Djedids spying for England, which they indeed did in Iran and Afghanistan.[143] However, suspicions of Djedids spying against Russia, most probably, were groundless. In archive materials on the Transcaspian oblast and on Turkestanskii krai as a whole, we did not find any facts of Djedid espionage for other countries, nor even their implication in it. To the contrary, an incident was mentioned in which a Djedid named Moshe Abramov gathered intelligence in Afghanistan for the Russian administration and was imprisoned in Herat for it. According to the Russian administration, M. Abramov was facing the death penalty, but he managed to break out of prison.[144] Upon that, he settled in Iolatan (Southern Turkmenia), according to a report of a Russian officer, "...before we came to Marv oasis".[145]

---

[140] TsGHAU, f. 1, op. 17, d. 922, pp. 62, 85; Naimark, 1889, p. 68.
[141] Leivi, 1930, pp. 17-18.
[142] TsGHAU, f. 1, op. 11, d. 1899, p. 1; там же, f. 1, op. 17, d. 922, p. 86; Trislov, 1902, no. 317; Patai, 1997, p. 119.
[143] Ieshua-Raz, 1992, p. 149-152; Levy, 1980, pp. 62-63; Netsar, 1990, p. 141.
[144] TsGHAU, f. 1, op. 17, d. 936, p. 333.
[145] Ibid.

Nevertheless, Djedids were very low-spirited about the imminence of their eviction.[146] Iranian Djedids attempted to conceal their devotion to Jewish tradition, since their families, with some minor exceptions, still were in Mashhad and they often came there on domestic and business matters. Despite the measures of secrecy they took, the Russian administration was aware of their devotion to Judaism.[147]

Although the Transcaspian oblast was included into the Turkestanskii krai in 1899, Djedids did not receive the status of "natives" as previously discussed. To a certain degree, this probably was because of a special temporary regulation that conferred wide autonomy upon the oblast chief. He was assigned many functions of a Governor-General.[148]

A law on eviction of Jews having citizenship of Asian countries adjacent with Turkestanskii krai was issued in 1900. It permitted continued residence in frontier towns of the Turkestanskii krai only for those of them who would enter the first or the second guild of merchants. Although the law would have come into force in 1906 (later, its coming into force was postponed until 1910), the chief of the Transcaspian oblast A.A. Bogoliubov (in office in 1899-1901) feared that many alien Jews would move to the near-border towns of Ashgabat and Marv. Therefore he, on the one hand, ordered the eviction of all Djedids that were Afghan citizens from Marv uezd until the beginning of 1904, and on the other hand – asked the Governor-General not to prohibit frontier towns in this oblast for Jews of this category to live in or to similarly prohibit their residence in Takhta-Bazar and Serakhs.[149] Vice-Governor-General

---

[146] The Jews in Merv, 1899.
[147] Ibid; Naimark, 1889, p. 64.
[148] Vremennoe polozhenie, 1911, pp. 941-943.
[149] TsGHAU, f. 1, op. 11, d. 1899, pp. 1-2; Ibid, f. 1, op. 17, d. 922, pp. 17, 86-86a.; Trislov, 1902, no. 317. At the time the eviction of Djedids of Afghan citizenship was going on, the chief administrator of the Marv uezd was given a permission to intercede for some of the exiles, to leave them in the uezd. TsGHAU, f. 1,

N.A. Ivanov did not agree with those suggestions, but not because he cared about Jews but because he saw them as a means to receive another special prerogative for governing his oblast, the Military governor of which already had broadened authority, as was said before.[150] As for the frontier towns in the Transcaspian oblast predestinated for Jews who were foreign citizens, Ivanov thought that since such towns were not defined in the law of 1900 and since the law did not mention that the local authorities should define them, Jews of this category could settle in all the settlements situated not far from the border, including the four above-mentioned settlements.[151]

A.N. Kuropatkin, who had become War Minister by that time and to whom A.A. Bogoliubov appealed because of the emerged disagreement, considered it best to consult S.Iu. Vitte, Minister of Finance. The Minister of Finance intended to protect Jews of the Transcaspian oblast from the restrictive effect of the law of 1900, but he had scant knowledge of the provisions of the Turkestanskii krai administration that allowed permanent residence of Jews of the adjacent countries. He responded by clarifying that the new law should not extend to the Transcaspian oblast. This argument of Vitte led to a quite undesirable result for him. The War Minister Kuropatkin pointed out to Ivanov, who by then had become Governor-General of Turkestanskii krai, that the above law should not be extended to this oblast at all and therefore alien Jews should not be accepted to live there at all, according to general Russian law.[152]

Following that, administrators of the Transcaspian oblast were governed by this law regarding Jews of Afghan and Iranian citizen-

---

op. 17, d. 922, p. 17.
[150] TsGHAU, f. 1, op. 11, d. 1899, p. 6.
[151] Ibid.
[152] TsGHAU, f. 1, op. 17, d. 922, pp. 86-86a. For this see also: Trislov, 1902, no. 318. Kuropatkin, who felt personal affection to the Transcaspian oblast, after having been appointed a War minister, kept de facto his full right of immediate control over the province, which had an adverse effect on the life of the local Jews.

ships.¹⁵³ D.I. Subbotich, who was the next Military governor after A.A. Bogoliubov (in office in 1901-1902,) planned to give effect to the decision on eviction of Djedids of Afghanistan citizenship from the Marv uezd of the Transcaspian oblast, but upon encountering resistance of a new chief of this uezd, F.A. Mikhailov, threw this scheme overboard.¹⁵⁴ V.V. Petrov, head of Tejen uezd, took the initiative to evict Jews of Iranian citizenship from his uezd, and D.I. Subbotich supported him in April 1902. Shortly afterwards, police gave the Djedids of Iranian citizenship corresponding letters of order.¹⁵⁵ Upon that, some Iranian Djedids scheduled to be evicted left the uezd. Probably, some of them went to Eretz-Israel to settle there, since according to Ben-Zion Ieshua-Raz, the first small wave of Djedid immigrants came there in 1903.¹⁵⁶ Aba Lev wrote that Djedids slated to be evicted avoided eviction by another conversion to Islam, this time the Sunni one, but this information cannot be proven.¹⁵⁷

V.V. Petrov, head of Tejen uezd, suspected Djedids in smuggling as well,¹⁵⁸ however, according to the Russian administration, not all Djedids smuggled, but the smugglers were not only Djedids, but also Turkmens, Iranians, and Russians.¹⁵⁹ Besides, Djedids themselves suffered from illicit trade, foremost from illicit traffic of tea to the Transcaspian oblast. Nikolai von der Hoffen, who was a civil servant in this oblast by the end of the 19ᵗʰ century and who reported the above fact, noted with sympathy that the Djedids who com-

---

¹⁵³ TsGHAU, f. 1, op. 17, d. 922, p. 86a.; Ibid, op. 13, d. 212, pp. 110-110a. It appears that F.A. Mikhailov's predecessor on that post, the orientalist G.A. Arendarenko, treated Jews with less tolerance.
¹⁵⁴ Ibid, op. 17, d. 922, pp. 64-64a.; Leivi, 1930, p. 18.
¹⁵⁵ TsGHAU, f.1, op.17, d. 922, pp. 4-5, 64, 87-88; Kaganovich, 1995, p. 125; Leivi, 1930, p. 18; Trislov, 1902, no. 318.
¹⁵⁶ Ieshua-Raz, 1992, p. 140.
¹⁵⁷ Lev, 1913.
¹⁵⁸ TsGHAU, f. 1, op. 17, d. 922, p. 64; Budushchnost', 1902.
¹⁵⁹ TsGHAU, f. 1, op. 17, d. 922, p. 64.

plained to him about that emphatically refused to give names, claiming to despise informing the authorities.[160]

Despite the above-mentioned letter of order, many Mashhadian Djedids stayed in the oblast since they were unable to conduct their businesses in Tejen within such a short term and were anticipated. They were arrested for disobedience,[161] but obviously were soon released. The Ministry of Foreign Affairs of Iran, which was indignant with this measure and with the expected eviction of Djedids, filed a protest that did not influence the intentions of the Russian administration,[162] and neither did a common request of 804 Salor Turkmens to leave all Djedids in Transcaspian oblast.[163] After that, Djedids themselves proffered four (!) requests to Nikolai II who agreed in 1903 to defer their eviction until the beginning of 1905 and then, in 1904, decided to pass this question over to the discretion of the local authorities.[164]

Iranian Djedids, by all methods possible, wished to defer their eviction from the Transcaspian oblast because they didn't want to end their successful commercial businesses, and feared persecution in their native country because they secretly observed Jewish traditions. They also wished to avoid the disorder and famine that started in Iran and in Mashhad particularly at the beginning of the 20th century.[165]

Probably, before the Pamir agreement was concluded in 1907 between Russia and England on dividing the spheres of influence in the Middle East, it was against Russian interests to evict Herati Jews

---

[160] Von der Hoffen, 1900, no. 26, p. 531.
[161] Leivi, 1930, p. 18.
[162] Amitin-Shapiro, 1933, p. 133; Leivi, 1930, p. 18.
[163] Leivi, 1930, p. 18; Trislov, 1902, no. 318.
[164] TsGHAU, f. 1, op. 17, d. 922, pp. 17a., 88; Voskhod, 1904. Curiously enough, Djedid wives presented one of the petitions to the Tsar in 1904. The women, needless to say, engaged in no activities, other than those that had to do with their household affairs, both before and after petitioning the monarch. TsGHAU, f. 1, op. 17, d. 922, pp. 88-88a.
[165] Ataev, 1989, pp. 15-17.

who led frontier trade. They were especially important for development of trade with Afghanistan, where Russian citizens couldn't enter. The arrest of Russian writer Vasilii Ian (Ianchievskii), who entered Afghanistan in 1903, was a clear evidence of this fact.[166] At the same time many Russian administrators who feared the strengthening of capitalism in Russia, which they associated with Jewish business activity, tended to retard the modernization with restrictive measures against Jews, primarily by restricting their residence. This position had an ideological background of preserving patriarchal and orthodox foundations of society that were headed by the Tsar's family.

At the same time, some Russian administrations favored not so much ideology as economic interests, and they found support the Ministry of Finance at the end of the 19th century and the beginning of the 20th century. One of these Russian administrators was E.E. Ussakovskii (in office in 1903-1905) who followed D.I. Subbotich. He was tolerant towards Herati and Mashhadi Jews, considering them to be useful for the oblast as a whole and especially for the development of trade with near-border regions of Afghanistan and Iran. Immediately after Kuropatkin, who disliked Jews, was dismissed from the position of War Minister in February 1904, Ussakovskii started to plead for Iranian Jews who lived in the Tejen uezd of the Transcaspian oblast. He strived for cancellation of their eviction or transferring them to a different uezd of the same oblast or, at least, postponement of their eviction.[167] Ussakovskii managed to attain the postponement by March 1904, but only for "useful Djedids".[168] A year later, in March 1905, touching on this question,

---

[166] Ian, 1989, vol. 4, p. 503.

[167] TsGHAU, f. 1, op. 17, d. 922, pp. 64-64a., 88a.; Kaganovich, 1995, pp. 125-126. Being accused of excessive liberalism in general and, as it might be, unwanted indulgence toward Jews, Ussakovskii was dismissed from his post of Military governor in 1905. The War ministry, on examining his case, retired him from the army. Rediger, 1999, vol. 2, pp. 16-17.

[168] TsGHAU, f. 1, op. 17, d. 922, p. 1; Ibid, d. 848, p. 91.

he wrote to the office of the Governor-General that he left all Djedids in the Tejen uezd since he could not elicit any facts of their "harmful activity".[169] Probably, it was thanks to Ussakovskii that on account of the eviction postponements of 1906 and 1908, the government privileges given to alien Jews living in the Turkestanskii krai were automatically given to Herati and Mashhadi Jews of the Transcaspian oblast, which the administrators initially had intended for Jews of Bukharan citizenship.[170] These postponements were attained by Bukharan Jews, their Moscow trading partners and Ministry of Finance.[171]

In February 1910 as Jews of Bukharan citizenship were evicted from the Transcaspian oblast, its new Military governor M.D. Evreinov (in office in 1907-1910) addressed a report to A.V. Samsonov in which he suggested the eviction of Djedids as well, as he believed that they, like Jews of Bukhara, "must equally be recognized as harmful elements for the oblast".[172] With that, Evreinov, who did not know local conditions, did not take into account the opinion of the Marv administration that eviction of Djedids would undermine trade in the uezd. Touching in his report on the economic role of Djedids he explained that they had already played their role in trade establishing economic ties with other countries and therefore they may be replaced.[173]

In the middle of July 1910 the Governor-General of Turkestanskii krai A.V. Samsonov supported the initiative of the military governor of the Transcaspian oblast to evict the Djedids from the oblast and ordered their eviction, providing them with one to two months to gather their belongings, depending on the period of their resi-

---

[169] Ibid, d. 922, p. 88a.
[170] Ibid, p. 89.
[171] Kaganovich, Attitude, 2003, pp. 120-121, 132-141.
[172] TsGHAU, f. 1, op. 17, d. 922, pp. 1-2; Novyi Voskhod, 1910, p.12; Rassvet, 1910, no. 29, p. 17. About the initiative of Evreinov see: Evreiskoe obozrenie, 1910.
[173] TsGHAU, f. 1, op. 17, d. 922, pp. 2-3.

dence in the oblast.[174] 563 Herati and Mashhadi Jews were subject to eviction: 309 Jews from Marv, 31 from Murgab, 23 from Takhta-Bazar and 210 from the Tejen uezd.[175] However, either because the time to gather belongings was too short or because approximately in August 1910 Evreinov was replaced with Iu. Zhukov (in office in 1910-1911) who was tolerant towards Jews, none of the alien Jews were evicted from the Transcaspian oblast. Eviction would just have been forgotten if it were not for rival traders of Djedids, the Armenians, who sent Samsonov a letter of denunciation.[176] The result was an order issued in the beginning of November 1910 for the immediate eviction of all alien Jews from the Transcaspian oblast.[177] When Iu. Zhukov passed that order to the head of Marv uezd F.I. Von Faler, he forgot to mention the actual deadline for the eviction.[178] The Marv administrator decided, probably in advance, to order the deportation of all Jews who resided in the oblast and who already were subject of eviction.[179]

Immediately after he learned about the forthcoming eviction of alien Jews, F.S. Milyashkevich, director of the Central-Asian department of the Russian-Chinese bank, made a stand for them in November 1910. He stated that Djedids and Jews of Bukharan citizenship were the most active in trade of the Marv uezd and that their eviction would result in material losses of the uezd population and banks, and besides "would kill trade of the Marv region with Iran and with Moscow for a long time".[180] Simultaneously, A.

---

[174] Evreiskoe obozrenie, 1910.

[175] Rassvet, 1910, no. 29, pp. 17-18. See also an excerpt from that article: Expulsion of Jews, 1910.

[176] Hazioni, 1913, p. 44; Vaisenberg, 1912, p. 404.

[177] TsGHAU, f. 1, op. 17, d. 922, pp. 62, 69; Kaganovich, 1995, p. 127.

[178] TsGHAU, f. 1, op. 17, d. 922, p. 62.

[179] Ibid. Jews of foreign citizenship, having been formally ordered by the Russian administration to end their stay in the Marv uezd, urgently sent a complaint addressed to N.M. Fridman, a deputy in the Duma, by telegraph. See: Rassvet, 1910, no. 46.

[180] TsGHAU, f. 1, op. 17, d. 922, p. 39.

Putilov, president of the Russian-Asian bank, upon receiving the news about this eviction from the director of the Samarkand department of the bank, told the Minister of Industry and Commerce that it would inflict serious losses upon them.[181]

The patriarchs of the Salor Turkmens of the Marv oasis and representatives of other Turkmenian aristocracy (some of whom had ranks of Russian senior officers) informed the administration that Turkmens always gave all their spare money to Herati and Mashhadi Jews who invested this money into different financial operations. With that, as they claimed, despite the fact that all money was given against no receipts – on parole – Jews never deceived any Turkmens. Turkmens asked the local administration to let the Jews remain at least temporarily so that they would not suffer losses from the cancellation of contracts Jews signed with banks and other companies.[182] Not being content with their petition to the Governor-General, Turkmens sent their request to the council of Ministers to postpone the eviction of Herati and Mashhadi Jews from the oblast.[183] The request of the Turkmens was supported by Iu. Zhukov, the Military governor of the Transcaspian oblast. He told the Governor-General of the Turkestanskii krai that Jews had lived among Turkmens even before the region was conquered and that they were among the founders of Russian Marv where they started their trade. Reporting about the large role that Bukharan and Afghan (Herati) Jews played in trade, Iu. Zhukov stated that they – unlike Armenians or Iranians – were honest in their bargains and possessed immovable property that had a total value of two million rubles. With that, the Military governor asked in case of impossibili-

---

[181] Russian Historical State Archive, St. Petersburg, f. 23, op. 25, d. 199, p. 59.

[182] TsGHAU, f. 1, op. 17, d. 922, pp. 42-45, 62a.; Expulsion from Bukhara, 1911; Hazioni, 1913, pp. 43-44; Kaganovich, 1995, pp. 128, 129; Rassvet, 1910, no. 50; Vaisenberg, 1912, p. 403.

[183] TsGHAU, f. 1, op. 17, d. 922, p. 74; Kaganovich, 1995, p. 129.

ty to leave Jews in the oblast, to grant the holders of immovable property six months for its sale.[184]
Jews of Bukharan and Afghan citizenships sent a telegram to N.M. Fridman, a delegate of the State Duma and an Ashkenazi Jew, in November 1910 where they reported about the order to be evicted within 24 hours. N.M. Fridman, in turn, immediately sent a telegram to the War Minister requesting to postpone the eviction.[185] During the same month, the Iranian consul in Ashgabat Djevad-Khan sent a letter to the officer responsible for boundary relations with the Transcaspian oblast, in which he stated that Djedids who were Iranian citizens observed Moslem traditions for several generations and even accomplished their pilgrimage to Mekka, therefore their eviction as Jews was an error.[186]
In November 1910, community leaders of Djedids to be evicted from the Marv uezd came to Tashkent in order to meet with the Governor-General, but evidently were not received by him. Therefore they had to send him a telegram with a request to call off the eviction.[187] Other representatives of Herati and Mashhadi Jews in the Transcaspian oblast sent another telegram to A.V. Samsonov during the same month.[188] However, the Governor-General, via his office, replied to all interceders with a refusal.[189] On December 11, 1910 he sent a telegram to the General Headquarters, in which he supported eviction of Jews from the Transcaspian oblast.[190] In return, N.G. Kondratyev, chief of the General Headquarters who supported eviction of alien Jews from another three oblasts of the Turkestanskii krai, expressed his doubt whether eviction of such

---

[184] TsGHAU, f. 1, op. 17, d. 922, pp. 62-63.
[185] Ibid, p. 41; Telegram from Merv, 1910.
[186] TsGHAU, f. 1, op. 17, d. 922, p. 65.
[187] Ibid, pp. 46-49.
[188] Ibid, p. 70.
[189] Ibid, p. 39a., 52-52a.; Kaganovich, 1995, p. 128.
[190] TsGHAU, f. 1, op. 17, d. 922, pp. 76-81.

Jews from the Transcaspian oblast was rational as he feared to further escalate the Jewish question in the pages of Russian newspapers and in the State Duma.[191]

However, in the beginning of January 1911, A.V. Samsonov, without waiting for the reply, gave the command to evict Jews of Afghanistan citizenship from the Marv uezd during that year, and also a majority of Jews of Iranian citizenship. He was actively supported by F.A. Shostak, the new head of the Transcaspian oblast who replaced Iu. Zhukov and was appointed by A.V. Samsonov.[192] As he shared the opinion of A.V. Samsonov that all Jews were a "harmful element for the oblast", he carefully asked the Governor-General of the Turkestanskii krai in April 1911 whether there was any legal basis for eviction of Djedids who officially professed Islam and who would even hide their commitment to Judaism more because of the eviction.[193] A.V. Samsonov replied that every Iranian citizen must be watched and "if his activity were found Jewish or if he were found to secretly observe Judaism – he must be evicted".[194]

Thus, formal profession of Djedids to Islam did not confuse the Governor-General of the Turkestanskii krai. He never took into account that according to Shariat law, Djedids would be facing death penalty in Iran since they observed Jewish traditions in the Transcaspian oblast. In the beginning of June 1911, 80 families of Herati and Mashhadi Jews in Marv, 40 families in Bairam-Ali, and

---

[191] Ibid, p. 139.

[192] Ibid, pp. 140, 141, 188; Expulsion of the Bukharan Jews, 1911; Hazioni, 1913, p. 43; Kaganovich, 1995, p. 130. As one may surmise, it is in 1911 that Jews of Iranian citizenship were banished out of the Syrdaria oblast. The fact that a petition filed by Khudaidat Tarakov, a Jew of Iranian citizenship, for permitting his stay in Chimkent in 1911, was rejected by the local authorities, helps us date the year of the banishment. See: TsGHAU, f. 17, op. 1, d. 11403, p. 2. Some Jews of Afghanistan citizenship managed to avoid the deportation by becoming Russian citizens. Thus, Moshe Abramov became, with the personal permission of the Tsar (Nikolai II), a Russian citizen, and was registered as a resident in Marv. See: TsGHAU, f. 1, op. 17, d. 978, p. 61.

[193] Ibid, d. 922, p. 171.

[194] Ibid.

125 families in Takhta-Bazar received evictions.[195] Only several dozens of Iranian Jewish families were left in the oblast, the ones who according to administrative data settled in the oblast before it was conquered in 1880. Despite the fact that beginning 1880 and until 1884 when Marv oasis was conquered, another 35 Djedid families moved there, they were evicted together with others in 1911.[196] The attitude of the Russian authorities towards Djedids was different from their attitude towards the above-mentioned Chalah Jews who escaped from Bukhara to Russian Turkestanskii krai and gained the right of residence there.[197] The reason for that was, on the one hand, that Russian legislature was more liberal towards Bukharan Jews than towards other sub-ethnic groups recognized in Russia as Jewish. On the other hand, the Emirate of Bukhara was under protectorate of Russia, and Russia felt politically responsible for events going on there, while a possible massacre of Jews in Iran was of little interest to Russia.

Probably, the majority of Herati and Mashhadi Jews who were evicted moved to Afghanistan.[198] Some of them did not even manage to sell their houses.[199] After eviction from the Transcaspian oblast, the local authorities let Jews of Afghanistan citizenship (and probably Iranian citizens) come there for business for three to four weeks every year. They tried to stay in the oblast for a longer period of time, but Russian officers kept strict watch on that.[200] In order to deceive Russian authorities and enter the Transcaspian oblast again, some Iranian Djedids changed their names to other, Moslem

---

[195] Rakhamim, 1911.
[196] TsGHAU, f. 1, op. 17, d. 922, p. 92. For Djedids living in Takhta-Bazar in 1913 see: Hazioni, 1913, p. 43.
[197] Kaganovich, 1997, pp. 70-75.
[198] This can be concluded, for instance, from the fact that all Djedids expelled from Takhta-Bazar went there. Hazioni, 1913, p. 43.
[199] Vaisenberg, 1916, p. 82.
[200] Hazioni, 1913, p. 43.

names.²⁰¹ Probably, Herati Jews also changed their names to Moslem ones. Some Herati Jews tried in 1912 to hold themselves out to be Karaims, since restrictions against Jews were not directed against Karaims. Unlike other Jews, alien Karaims could enter Russia and live there.²⁰² But even that could not help Yehuda and his father Djura Iglanov, rich Jews from Marv, to stay in the Turkestanskii krai. They were refused by the Russian authorities²⁰³ since the authorities must have known that Karaims did not live in Afghanistan or in Iran at that time. Yehuda Iglanov gained the right to live in the Russian colony in the Emirate of Bukhara (in the town of Novaia Bukhara, now called Kagan) only several years later, after he and his wife fictitiously converted to Lutheranism. After the February Revolution of 1917 in Russia, the family officially returned to Judaism.²⁰⁴

Herati and Mashhadi Jews who emigrated to the territory of the Samarkand oblast before beginning of the 1870s were recognized as "natives", and the majority of the ones who came there later apparently changed their citizenship to Bukharan in the end of the 19th century or in the beginning of the 20th century and until 1917 lived in Samarkand as Jewish citizens of Bukhara in peril of being evicted to the Emirate by the Russian administration for any small infraction.²⁰⁵

---

[201] Vaisenberg, 1916, p. 82.
[202] Laws on conditions, 1899, paragraph 818, p. 106.
[203] TsGHAU, f. 1, op. 13, d. 821, p. 9.
[204] TsGHAU, f. 3, op. 2, d. 900, p. 1.
[205] In 1897 Adler found both in Bukhara and Samarkand several Djedid families having a permanent residence there. Adler, Jews in Many Lands, 1905, p. 214. For the three Djedids – two from Afghanistan and the other one from Marv – living in Samarkand in 1894 see: TsGHAU, f. 18, op. 1, d. 4468, p. 54. For the three Jews of Iranian citizenship living in Samarkand in 1900 see: TsGHAU, f. 18, op. 1, d. 4462, pp. 15-16. For the family of Simkha-Agadjan Israilov, a Djedid who traded in Marv and lived in Samarkand in 1911, see: TsGHAU, f. 18, op. 1, d. 4929, pp. 9, 34. For the Djedid migration to Samarkand, Kokand and Tashkent see: Kupovetskii, 1992, p. 57.

Bukharan Djedids in the Turkestanskii krai, just like Herati and Mashhadi Jews who stayed in the Transcaspian oblast, were subject to jurisdiction by Moslem courts, not regular state courts,[206] since the Russian administration did not want to interfere with customs of the Central Asia oblasts that existed there before they had been conquered by Russia, especially customs regarding alien Jews.[207]

Socio-Economic Life

Mashhadi Jews who had settled in Turkmenia became, over time, principal mediators in the trade with neighboring countries, mainly with Iran where they could have come in the guise of Shi'ites and where Turkmens were particularly disliked. The reason of such attitude to Turkmens lay in their bad repute as caravan robbers, rather than in their being Sunnis.[208] Even in Central Asia where caravan robbery was a common thing, Turkmen plunderers were known for their daring attacks. Moreover, Turkmens used to maraud the nearby outskirts of Iran, to capture slaves whom they subsequently sold to slave-traders from Bukhara. No exceptions were made even for Sunni prisoners, the slave-traders' co-religionists, who became objects of that notorious trade, to much indignation of the Islamic clergy of Bukhara. Few caravan traders, therefore, were bold enough to set out for a ride to Turkmenia. In return, Turkmen traders (it was a small social group, so called *charva* – mainly of Turkmen Tekkes – that engaged in trading)[209] were at constant risk of revenge by the prisoners' kinsmen when abroad.

---
[206] Central Historical State Archive of Ukraine, Kiev, f. 1004, op. 1, d. 100, p. 158 [copy located in the Central Archive of the History of the Jewish People, Jerusalem (HM2/7953)].
[207] Kaganovich, Attitude, 2003, pp. 292-293, 313.
[208] This was written about by a number of travelers and explorers. See, for example: Entner, 1965, p. 2; Naimark, 1889, pp. 67-68; Tikhomirov, 1960, pp. 71-73.
[209] Tikhomirov, 1960, p. 30.

Besides, the frequent wars that Turkmen tribes waged against the neighboring countries hampered the progress of Turkmen foreign trade. In the first half of the 19th century relations between Turkmen tribes and Iranian Qajars were especially tense, on account of the numerous attempts made to subjugate them.[210]

The need for mediators in trade must have protected Jews from being turned into slaves, although Arminius Vambery believed it was thanks to the opinion the Moslems of Central Asia had, that Jews were useless as slaves. However, he was probably right when he wrote that Turkmens also had a superstitious fear of Jews – reputed sorcerers and magicians.[211] Henry Lansdell, an English traveler, noted that Djedids, normally, lived there under the auspices of one Turkmen or another.[212] At the same time, Mashhadi and Herati Jews played an important role in regional trade, providing Turkmens with all necessary goods.[213] Commercial relations that Jews had in the region made it possible for them to be mediators in cases where Russians or Iranians needed to ransom their relatives from captivity,[214] and this fact vouches for their weight in regional trade. Edmond O'Donovan, who lived for a couple of years in the oasis of Marv in the early 1880s, mentioned in his book the fact that Djedids pursued trade – wholesale and retail – with all kinds of goods, from silk and cotton fabrics to medicines and copper utensils.[215] To the knowledge of C.E. Stewart, an English officer who visited the oasis of Marv at that time, most merchants in the bazar near the Turkmen camp on the Murghab river were Jews. The bazar used to be open twice a week.[216]

---

[210] See, for example: Kuznetsova, 1983, pp. 116-124.
[211] Vambery, 1877, p. 280.
[212] Lansdell, 1885, vol. 2, p. 479.
[213] Von der Hoffen, 1900, no. 26, p. 530.
[214] Ibid.
[215] O'Donovan, 1882, vol. 2, pp. 152, 379.
[216] Stewart, 1977, p. 150.

Some officials of the Russian administration, as was already mentioned, favored participation of Herati Jews in the Russian-Afghan trade. Herati Jews imported dried fruit, wool and hides (astrakhan, mostly) from Afghanistan into Russia.[217] According to the 1891 statistics, the Herati Jews of only the Marv uezd sent those goods to Russia for as much as 670,000 roubles during that year.[218] It was quite a considerable sum taking into account the prices of that time, even if the goods really belonged to both Herati and Mashhadi Jews: Russian officials who were not always precise in their classification of ethnic groups[219] might have registered all Djedid traders as "Herati Jews". The total trade turnover of Marv in 1887 was 1 million roubles – the figure that makes one understand how great the role of Djedids was in the uezd trade.[220] In Russia, Herati Jews purchased cotton, silk and woolen fabrics, to send them with caravans to Herat via Takhta-Bazar, a border town. At the border the camels (the most commonly used caravan pack-animals of Central Asia) were replaced with donkeys, since the further part of the way came through passes in mountains. The caravan drivers themselves rode horses both in mountains and on plain.[221] Jewish traders brought to Herat big sums in golden Russian roubles,[222] which means that they imported more goods to Russia than they brought back. Caravan trading was not a safe thing due to the attacks of Afghan bandits who sometimes made ambushes on the way. A Saint-Petersburg paper wrote of one of such incident

---

[217] Obzor, 1893, p. 270.
[218] Ibid.
[219] About a fact of erroneous reckoning of Djamshedis among Djedids see: Ts-GHAU, f. 1, op. 17, d. 922, p. 64.
[220] Tikhomirov, 1960, p. 202.
[221] Svet, 1907. The total amount of cotton cloths of all kinds, imported to Afghanistan from Russia in 1913, equaled 1,745 tons. Zashchuk, 1928, p. 226. It seems highly probable that Herati Jews brought a considerable part of that cloth into Afghanistan.
[222] Svet, 1907.

that took place in 1907: a caravan of sixteen Herati Jewish traders and several drivers fell victim to armed Afghan robbers on its way back to Herat. The robbers attacked the caravan on Russian territory. They wounded five of the traders and the guide with swords, took all money that the caravan had – 18,000 golden roubles and 5,000 Iranian krans – and robbed the best of its goods.[223] On territory of Afghanistan robberies were no unusual occurrence, either, especially up to the end of the 19th century.[224] Armenians of Russian citizenship were reluctant to come to Afghanistan with caravans, since visiting that country was rather dangerous for them until the aforementioned treaty between the Russian and the British Empires was signed. Herati Jews had yet other competitors in that trade – Moslems from Bukhara[225] whose legal status was more preferable in Afghanistan and in the Emirate of Bukhara: unlike Herati Jews who had the status of Dhimmis, they did not pay double trade tax, or *zakāt*.[226] On the other hand the double *zakāt* imposed upon Jews, probably, made their trade in opinion of the Afghani authorities more preferable. Besides, taking into account that the Afghani governors, and in particular emir Abder-Rahman Khan (ruled from 1880 till 1901), oppressed foreign merchants because they wanted to develop national trade,[227] possibly, Herati Djedids also enjoyed a most favored status. Enjoying this support, and also some tolerance of the Russian administration towards Jews of Afghanistan citizenship, as mentioned above, Herati Djedids had taken strong positions in the Russian-Afghani trade. Owing to them, at the end of the 19th century, Russian fab-

---

[223] Ibid.
[224] Babakhodzhaev, 1975, p. 56.
[225] Ibid, p. 55.
[226] Zakāt – in its prime meaning: alms tax, collected for charity needs, with regard for the material status and profession of the taxpayer; with time, it changed into a cattle tax, a tax on property in general and on goods for sale in particular. The official rate of zakāt for Moslems was 2.5%. Ivanov, 1954, p. 38; Khoroshkhin, 1876.
[227] Babakhodzhaev, 1975, pp. 68-71.

rics put an end to the British-Indian monopoly on fabrics about which Soviet orientalist Babakhodzhaev wrote.[228] According to his data, during five years, from 1897 to 1901 the share of cotton fabrics in total exports of Russian goods to Afghanistan grew from 56% up to 85%.[229]

The rate of *zakāt* in Afghanistan, more likely than not, was one twentieth for Dhimmis and one fortieth for Moslems.[230] As a matter of fact, the extortionists of the officials forced all traders, Moslems and non-Moslems alike, to pay much higher taxes.[231] In 1912, the merchants committee of Kokand raised the question of reining in and regulating tax-collection in Afghanistan,[232] but apparently, the question found no solution.

To a lesser degree the Russian authorities were interested in Mashhadi Jews participating in the Russian-Iranian trade. Traditionally, the Russians relied on their Armenian allies in Iran; hence Russia protected Armenian interests in its trade policy in that region. Armenians of Russian and Iranian citizenship traded mostly in the Iranian provinces of Astrabad, Mazanadaran and Gilan, while trade in the Khorassan province was neglected, due to its remoteness from Central Russia.[233] It was in that province that Mashhadi Jews became, by the beginning of the 20th century, a

---

[228] Ibid, p. 72.
[229] Ibid.
[230] For imposing on Bukharan Jews a 5% zakāt see, for instance: Abreq, 1887, p. 2; News from Borders of Israel, 1862; The report made in 1907 by the Andijan uezd chief administrator on the legal status of Bukharan Jews under the Khans see in: TsGHAU, f. 19, op. 1, d. 28792, p. 3. At the same time, in Moslem Kashgar Jews and Hindus were forced to pay a 10% zakāt – four times higher than the tax Moslems normally paid. Valikhanov, 1986, p. 192.
[231] Ivanov, 1954, p. 38; Khoroshkhin, 1876.
[232] Kokand Stock Exchange Committee, 1912, p. 102.
[233] For the role Armenians played in the Russian-Iranian trade and for the protectionist policy of Russia towards Iranian Armenians see: Kuznetsova, 1980, pp. 118, 122-123, 126; Kuznetsova, 1983, pp. 140-141, 146, 185-188; Kazembeyki, 2003, p. 111-114. For Russian goods which came to Khorassan through Astrabad by the 70s of the 19th century see: Venyukov, 1877, p. 71.

noticeable factor in Russian trade with Iran. The trade was helped a lot by the construction of the Transcaspian railroad, which in 1886 linked Marv to the coastal area of the Caspian Sea. The railroad construction greatly stimulated the development of that trade in general: it drew part of the trade flow from traditional roadways connecting inner areas of Iran with the southern coast of Caspian Sea and directed it to Khorassan, only some dozen kilometers from the railroad.[234] As a result, Mashhad became a large hub on the trade route between Russia and Iran.[235] Many Armenians of Russian citizenship, eager to regain their position in the trade, flocked to the Transcaspian oblast in the 1880s; there were 8,414 of them living in the oblast by 1908.[236] Many of them engaged in commerce,[237] rivaling, as traders, the local Mashhadi Jews.[238] It was not easy for Armenian traders to supplant their Jewish competitors, though, because of the right of settlement the latter had in the Transcaspian oblast at that time, together with Iranian citizenship that entitled them to own real estate,[239] and the status of Moslems, to boot, which meant paying only half as much zakāt – all putting the local Jews in a wonderful competitive position, especially in the field of long distance trade with Iran and Central Russia. On their visits to Russia, Mashhadi Jews mostly stayed in Moscow and Nizhnii Novgorod Fair.[240] The success they achieved in trade

---

[234] For the development of the Russian-Iranian trade via Khorassan at the end of the 19th – the beginning of the 20th century see: Ataev, 1971, pp. 14-18; Ataev, 1989, p. 75; Entner, 1965, p. 52. For the drastic rise in the Russian-Iranian trade starting in 1888 see: Entner, 1965, pp. 8-9.

[235] Ataev, 1989, p. 75; Mannanov, 1962, p. 49; Entner, 1965, pp. 25, 75. By construction of the Zakaspijskoj road, the significant part of barter between Afghanistan and Russia through disappeared Babakhodzhaev, 1965, p. 65.

[236] Russian Historical State Archive, St. Petersburg, f. 1396, op. 1, d. 172, p. 76.

[237] For the important role of Armenians in the regional trade see: TsGHAU, f. 22, op. 1, d. 1063, p. 73; Ataev, 1989, p. 77.

[238] Obzor, 1893, pp. 27-29, 271; Trislov, 1902, no. 318.

[239] For foreign possession of real estate having been banned in Iran see: Entner, 1965, p. 15.

[240] Naimark, 1889, pp. 63, 65; Benari, 1910; Von der Hoffen, 1900, no. 26, p. 530.

stimulated a new wave of Jewish immigration from Khorassan and Afghanistan to Turkmenia during the first decade of the 20th century. However, as soon as Djedids were expelled from Turkmenia, their positions in business went over to Armenians. Thus, the expulsion of Jews from Serakhs in 1902-1903 resulted in immediate growth of the number of shops owned by Armenians – from three to five.[241]

The main exports from Iran to Russia were dried fruit, raw cotton, rice, skins and carpets; cotton fabrics and sugar comprised 75% of the import from Russia to Iran until World War I. The choice of those goods as main import articles was dictated by the customs policy of the Russian authorities that, in their attempts to oust goods of European fabrication from markets of Khorassan, freed some kinds of Russian products from tax.[242] In the early 1890s, Mashhadi Jews (in co-operation with Bukharan Jews) practiced intense commercial exchange with manufacturers in the Moscow industrial zone,[243] sending them raw cotton from Iran, to bring back textiles in exchange. The amount of Russian textile production that was imported to Khorassan in the very end of the 19th century equaled a 2.3 million roubles.[244]

Herati and Mashhadi Jews from the Transcaspian oblast, needing credits for wholesale trade operations, approached the Turkmen tribal aristocracy for loans;[245] the aristocrats were ready to give credits to Jews, getting a high interest on the loans. In most cases the loans granted were not in money, but in cotton that was subsequently sent to Russia, to be sold there. Thus, in 1910,

---

[241] Turkestanskie Vedomosti, 1905.
[242] Zashchuk, 1928, pp. 226-227; Mannanov, 1962, pp. 48, 50; Entner, 1965, pp. 24, 67-72, 78; Ataev, 1971, p. 14-15.
[243] About the close relations the Bukharan Jewish businessmen had with the Moscow textile manufacturers see: Kaganovich, Attitude, 2003, pp. 77, 82, 120.
[244] Obzor, 1900, c. 181.
[245] Vaisenberg, 1912, p. 404.

Djedids were credited 200,000 "poods" (3,200 tons) of cotton.[246] On the other hand, some Turkmens borrowed money from Herati and Mashhadi Jews. In 1902, for instance, Salor Turkmens of the Serakhs *pristavstvo* were given 16,000 roubles as a credit; the creditor was Khuda-Bakhsh Sulemanov, a Djedid.[247] Farajullah Narulayoff mentioned in his memoirs giving credits to Turkmens, against the next-season crop of cotton.[248]

On the whole, the primary article of export brought by Herati and Mashhadi Djedids from Turkmenia (mainly from the Marv uezd and, probably, from the Tejen uezd) to Central Russia and Bukhara was cotton. The other goods they sent there were mostly skins, wool, dried fruit and flour.[249] From Central Russian and Iran, they brought Russian and especially Iranian cloths for Turkmens living in the Transcaspian oblast, the Iranian cloths being most desirable for their better quality.[250] Besides that, Djedids supplied the inhabitants of Turkmenia and Bukhara with Russian sugar.[251] The main trading centers of the Marv uezd were the bazars of Marv, Iolatan and Takhta-Bazar. The bazar in Marv – the biggest of the three – had 352 shops. Its market days gathered up to five thousand visitors.[252] The fact that the three chief managers of the bazar were a Tatar, an Armenian and a Djedid makes it obvious that many shop-keepers there were Djedids.[253] G.P. Miller, describing his visit to Marv in the late 1880s, wrote that at that bazar, Djedid merchants sold "virtually everything: from pheasants

---

[246] TsGHAU, f. 1, op. 17, d. 922, p. 44.
[247] Trislov, 1902, no. 317.
[248] Patai, 1997, p. 143.
[249] Obzor, 1893, p. 270; Patai, 1997, p. 135; TsGHAU, f. 1, op. 17, d. 922, p. 44.
[250] Turkestanskie Vedomosti, 1905.
[251] Patai, 1997, p. 135.
[252] Obzor, 1893, pp. 270-271.
[253] Despite the fact that the author told of a Jew, not Djedid, it is likely (judging from what was told above) that he meant a Djedid. We cannot exclude also that by "Tartar" he meant a Turkmen. Tikhomirov, 1960, p. 165.

and camels to three-piece suits and [European – A.K.] hats".[254] According to the information that Nikolai von der Hoffen submitted in 1900, many Djedids, having no more than 2-3 thousand roubles in cash, managed to carry on trades with turnovers as high as tens of thousand roubles: they delivered their goods, mainly wool and astrakhan, to the biggest Russian fair of Nizhny Novgorod, where they bought cloths, not only with the cash they had at the time, but largely on credit. The textile manufacturers of Central Russia preferred Djedids to Moslems as customers, and appreciated their "accuracy and efficiency in business".[255] Big Moslem businessmen showed much preference for Djedids as well.[256]

Many Djedids in the Transcaspian oblast made fortunes rapidly at that time.[257] Although the expulsion of those who had no Russian citizenship ruined some businesses, many of the deportees, living now in northern parts of Afghanistan and Iran, continued with the intermediate trade they had engaged in before and went to Russia as visiting aliens. Thus, the 66-year-old Djedid rabbi of Mashhad, Mordekhai (Murad) Ahalar (Ahlarov), went on a business trip to Moscow in 1916 – an example showing how important the trade with Russia was to Djedids.[258] Some foreign family clans of Djedids had their family businesses in Marv or another town in Turkestan run by a secret representative, usually a close relative, who was from time to time replaced by another member of the clan so that the local Russian authorities would not know of the arrangement. F. Narulayoff, for instance, would spend 15-16 consecutive months in Marv, the main residence of their family business, and then one

---

[254] Miller, 1909, p. 890. Though Miller in his memoirs called the Jews Bukharan, he probably had Djedids in mind, we assume, taking into account the number of representatives each of the two sub-ethnic groups had in Marv at that time.
[255] Von der Hoffen, 1900, no. 26, pp. 530-531.
[256] Ibid, p. 531.
[257] Vaisenberg, 1916, p. 82.
[258] Fuzailov, Rabbis, 1995, p. 109; Ieshua-Raz, 1992, p. 125-126.

of his brothers would come and replace him. All of them were merchants in Mashhad, Bukhara, Kaakha and the Iranian town of Darrehgaz, and had families and children there.[259] The company that belonged to the Narulayoff family was of average capital and commercial activity. Perhaps the biggest Djedid family business belonged to the Aminov brothers. The clan representatives escaped deportation from Takhta-Bazar and Marv, where they owned a big warehouse. The Aminovs had subsidiaries in Mashhad, Teheran and Nizhny Novgorod fair. Their company held strong positions in the region's wholesale trade in raw cotton, textiles, wool, silk and leather goods.[260] Another big trading company belonged to Yehuda Iglanov (of whom also see above) and his father Djura. The company built a cotton gin factory in Marv in the beginning of the 20th century.[261]

The formation of Djedid family enterprises can be dated back to the middle of the 19th century. Such enterprises normally would have their representatives in Mashhad and somewhere in Turkmenia (Marv was the most likely place beginning in the middle of the 1880s). As trade developed in the beginning of the 20th century, the largest family companies would have representatives in several Central Asian towns, such as Bukhara, Samarkand, Kokand, and in Moscow. Family companies of Bukharan Jews of Central Asia had similar networks of their representatives in different towns of the Turkestanskii krai, in Central Russia, and in Bukhara.[262]

Payments in this trade were made in Iranian silver coins – krans (one kran was equal to 0.18 rouble) – not only in Mashhad, but in the Transcaspian oblast as well. These coins were popular among

---

[259] Patai, 1997, pp. 135-145.
[260] Konopka, 1912, p. 22. The Mashhadi rabbi Benyamin Aminov was possibly related to the family. See about him: Fuzailov, Rabbis, 1995, p. 106. Djedids from Mashhad, on their visits to Teheran, were bold enough to stay in the Jewish quarter and observe Jewish religious laws. Abezgauz, 1904, p. 109.
[261] Turkmenistan, 1996, p. 1104.
[262] Kaganovich, Attitude, 2003, pp. 48, 141, 229-233.

the local population of the Transcaspian oblast since export from Iran and Afghanistan to Russia was greater than import, as mentioned before. Iranian Djedids played a prominent role in the contraband import of these coins to Russia (the only way possible).[263] They, as well as other merchants participating in Russian-Iranian trade, must have exported in return the Russian silver roubles that were popular in Iran.[264]

During World War I, especially in 1915-1916, Djedids of Afghanistan and Iranian citizenships, who lived in Takhta-Bazar and Tashkepri (both in the Marv uezd, near the Afghanistan border) began to export more Russian silver roubles to Iran and to Afghanistan. They sold them for Russian note money, the rate of exchange being 1:1,4-1,5, to local banks and merchants that found themselves in a devaluation fever. It was done in an underhand way, as the Russian government, because of its suspiciousness and espionage hysteria, considered smuggling to be an economic diversion in favor of Germany.[265]

Djedid merchants reached their heyday at the end of the 19th century and the first decade of the 20th century. This can be understood from the fact that 8 of the 202 Djedid adult men belonged to the first guild of merchants and 129 more – to the second one, as they were engaged mainly in mediatory trade between Russia, Bukhara and Iran.[266] Besides, the number of stone houses that Djedids owned in Marv, increased from 46 (8.6% of all houses in the town) in 1900[267] to 112 in 1910[268], in spite of the threat of evic-

---

[263] TsGHAU, f. 1, op. 17, d. 922, pp. 17, 64; Trislov, 1902, no. 317. For Aminov brothers' trading in Iranian krans see: Dmitriev-Mamonov, 1912, c. 27. About smuggling krans into Russia see: Ataev, 1989, pp. 77-78; Entner, 1965, p. 62. For the kran rate see: Ataev, 1989, p. 41.
[264] Entner, 1865, pp. 43-44.
[265] TsGHAU, f. 461, op. 1, d. 1885, pp. 13-34; d. 2329, p. 375a.
[266] Ibid, f. 1, op. 17, d. 848, pp. 79-85.
[267] Obzor, 1902, p. 138.
[268] TsGHAU, f. 1, op. 17, d. 848, pp. 79-85; Obzor, 1902, p. 138.

tion. In another place of the Marv uezd, Iolantan, the number of stone houses decreased from 11 (25% of all houses)[269] to 3.[270] By 1910, Djedids of the Tejen uezd had 57 stone and brick houses including 20 in Serakhs and 37 in Chaacha.[271]

To sum up, by 1910, the real estate property of Mashhadi and Herati Djedids in the Transcaspian oblast (mainly houses and shops) was worth 2 million roubles[272], which was a considerable amount of money by then. We should, however, take into consideration that purchase of real estate was not a goal but a necessity: First, Djedids were under threat of eviction (which could have been attended with unprofitable sales). Second, they stood in need of a means to increase trade turnover; and third, many of them spent money to support their families who were left in Afghanistan and Iran because of their fear of eviction. Thus, the valuation of Djedids' real estate does not show the real level of their wealth. In view of all these considerations it was much higher. According to the official data of the office of the Governor-General, the common annual trade turnover of Djedids in 1910 was 3,680 million roubles.[273] Most likely, about 3 million roubles of the above sum were the result of cotton resale transactions. This follows from the above mentioned credit given to Djedids for 200,000 poods of cotton, from probable purchase of cotton for cash as well, and from the fact that the average price for Bukharan cotton in 1910 was 13.5 rouble per pood[274] (Bukharan cotton was the variety that was grown in Turkmenia and Afghanistan and was cheaper than the American variety of cotton grown in the Fergana valley). Taking into account that the same year's export of cotton

---

[269] Obzor, 1902, p. 138.
[270] Obzor, 1913, p. 339.
[271] TsGHAU, f. 1, op. 17, d. 848, p. 94; Obzor, 1913, p. 338.
[272] TsGHAU, f. 1, op. 17, d. 922, p. 52a.
[273] Ibid, d. 849, p. 86.
[274] Statistical yearbook, 1914, pp. 646-647.

from the Transcaspian oblast to Central Russia was about one million pood,[275] the share of Djedids was rather considerable: 22.2%.

Some Djedids living in the Transcaspian oblast were involved in handicrafts.[276] It is most likely that they made clothing and footwear. They also may have dyed fabric as Bukharan Jews did.[277]

After the Bolshevik revolution in Russia in 1917, many Mashhadi and Herati Jews continued trading under the circumstances of economic decline that were caused by the revolution, civil war and Bolsheviks' measures against merchants. During "NEP" ("New Economic Policy"), in 1921-1927 the economy revived again. Having visited Central Asia in 1923, the English communist Ralph Fox wrote of its economy, "This was the heyday of NEP and all Russia was like America in the early forties. Men were in fever to grow rich, to win back what the Revolution had taken...".[278] As was mentioned above, many Mashhadi and Herati Jews returned to the Transcaspian oblast and other regions of Turkmenistan in order to remain in business. After the state power in the USSR got stronger it started to cut down NEP by means of nationalization and extremely high taxes for business. As a result, many Mashhadi and Herati Jews incurred significant losses. Some of them returned to Afghanistan and Iran, as mentioned above. It is worth mentioning Abdul Kerim (Rahamim) Itshakov as an example of the situation prevailing at that time. He was occupied with trade in Marv and Samarkand, and, during the late 1920s, in Moscow. But because of high taxes in the USSR he was forced to go back to Mashhad where

---

[275] Kokand Stock Exchange Committee, 1913, pp. 16-17. As much as 9.4 million poods of cotton in total were exported in 1910 into Central Russia from Central Asia, including the Emirate of Bukhara. Ibid.
[276] The Jews in Merv, 1899.
[277] Zand, 1990, p. 536.
[278] Fox, 1925, p. 77.

he became the head of the Djedid community, which he remained until he died in 1937.[279]

At the end of the 1920s and during the early 1930s, the state monopoly for trade was implemented, which aggravated the situation in USSR. Many Mashhadi and Herati Jews, obviously, were involved in smuggling on both sides of the border, and this eased for them, to a certain extent, the negative consequences of the nationalization of economy in the USSR. The shortage of goods in Soviet Russia induced smuggling. For instance, Nataniel Eliaghu who lived in Kerki until the early 1930s, was a smuggler and brought there from Afghanistan green tea, gauze, paints and other goods, which he exchanged for gold.[280] Obviously, the same kinds of goods were brought by Mashhadi and Herati Jews from Iran and Afghanistan. In general, smuggling, mainly to and from Iran, gained in scope during the late 1920s not only in the near-border area where most Mashhadi and Herati Jews lived, but in Turkmenia in general. Mainly tea, perfume, and opium were brought to Turkmenia, while karakul guts, carpets, kerosene, and other goods were taken out.[281] Most likely, by the middle of the 1930s, when both Soviet and Afghanistan governments succeeded to close their borders, smuggling decreased.[282]

Thus, by the middle of the 1930s Mashhadi and Herati Jews of Iran and Afghanistan lost all opportunities to trade with Russia through

---

[279] Asherov, 1977, p. 155.

[280] Interview of Moshe Mossek with Nataniel Eliahu, September 5, 1974, Oral History Archive of the Institute of Contemporary Jewry, the Hebrew University of Jerusalem, No. 16 (54), tape 682 k.

[281] Aitakov, 1929, c. 67. About the wide-spread participation of Mashhadi and Herati Jews in an illicit trade through the Soviet border with Turkmenia see: Dilmanian, 1997, p. 77.

[282] Interview with Iehuda Kohen, May 12, 2006 (from the author's own archive). The Bukharan Jews of Central Asia used to come to Turkmenia and cross the border there; the border crossing came to an end in the middle 1930s, which gives evidence of the border being closed at that time. Many fugitives were arrested at that period. Fuzailov, From Bukhara to Jerusalem, 1995, pp. 255-262, 267-268; Koplik, 2003, pp. 355-357.

Turkmenia. The largest communities of Djedids in Mashhad and Herat were deprived from their most important source of livelihood. They faced a new urgent problem: to find another way to earn their living. Many Mashhadi and Herati Jews upon leaving the USSR settled in Herat and other Afghanistan towns, not far from Turkmenia. They started trading in karakul skins, cotton articles and sugar with European countries. However, after Abdul Madjid Khan implemented a monopoly for this trade, Djedids had no choice but to leave. Many Mashhadi and Herati Jews of Iran and Afghanistan did not find any way to earn their livings in their home towns; they preferred emigration to Eretz Israel and Western Europe[283] to religious discrimination they suffered from in their motherland, although the discrimination at the time was not overt. Years of living in the territory of Russian Empire where Iranian Djedids could almost freely return to Judaism and where Afghan Djedids were secure from pogroms made their spirits strong. The social status of merchants that Djedids had in Russia contributed to their spiritual liberation and strengthening of their Jewish self-identity, helping them forget the feeling of a haunted victim they had had until then. This conclusion, which we consider to be valid as well, was made by Rafael Patai who researched the past of Mashhadi Jews during the 1940s in numerous interviews.[284]

Communal and Religious Life

Having taken their residence in Turkmen settlements in the second third of the 19th century, Mashhadi and Herati Jews succeeded in

---

[283] Forbes, 1940, p. 58; Dilmanian, 1997, p. 76-77; Fuzailov, Rabbis, 1995, pp. 111-112.

[284] Patai, 1946, p. 218. The article contains curious information about Djedids teaching their children Jewish religion and Hebrew secretly in Mashhad through the period from the last third of the 19th century until the early 1940s.

arranging communal life of their own and observing religious rituals within the framework of united communities. As it was already mentioned, the local Moslem authorities put no obstacles in their ways. According to O'Donovan, wine and vodka, consumed while celebrating Jewish festivals, was pby Jews in Marv and, apparently, other towns as well, and Moslems knew about that.[285]

The mass arrival of the Russians at the end of the 19th and the beginning of the 20th century brought the united community of Herati and Mashhadi Jews to a formal split. The reason for this lay in the fact that Mashhadi Jews, apprehensive of a possible banishment as they were, resumed demonstrating their devotion to Islam in public and denying their Jewish origin. The local newspaper *Askhabad* wrote in those days that in the presence of Moslems they strictly observed the Mohammedan fast of Ramadan, attended prayer services in mosques and gave money to the poor on the Shi'ite mourning day Shahsei-Wahsei (commemorating the death of Imam Hussein – Caliph Ali's son).[286]

The same paper stated, however, that Iranian Djedids living in Marv almost never went to the mosque on week-days, prayed secretly in the Bukharan Jews' synagogue [most likely, it was an Afghan Djedids' synagogue that was meant here – A.K.] or in a secret beth-midrash of theirs. They did not sell things on Saturdays, leaving servant boys in their shops who would tell potential customers that the boss temporarily went out of the shop. They did not buy meat unless it was of Jewish shekhita, nor did they marry Moslems other than from their own circle, or took as wives Jewish girls from families openly professing Judaism, which was not illegal

---

[285] O'Donovan, 1882, vol. 2, p. 129.

[286] Trislov, 1902, no. 317. For other quotations from the article see also: Budushchnost', 1902; Voskhod, 1902. The author calls the holiday Uraza, though Uraza Bairam, or 'Id al-fitr' in Arabic, is, in fact, a feast breaking the month-long fast of Ramadan. Shahsey-Wahsey (from the Persian: "Shah Hussein, wah Hussein") is called a feast incorrectly.

by Shari'at law.[287] Samuil Vaisenberg mentioned in 1916 that some Djedid males in the Transcaspian oblast were living in marital cohabitation with Bukharan or Iranian Jewish wives, no violation of Shari'at law being found with the case. The reason for such marriages, in his opinion, was that they made it possible for a Djedid husband, if being accused of neglecting Mohammedan traditions, to blame his wife for it, thus exonerating himself.[288] By 'Iranian Jewish wives' the author probably meant Herati Jewesses, as we may assume on the grounds that there were no Iranian Jews other than of Mashhadi origin, living in the province, with a possible exception for several families that came from Teheran. It was already mentioned before that many Djedids left their wives and children back in Mashhad, Herat and other places in Afghanistan. The adult males came to see their families on Jewish holidays, such as Passover or Succoth.

The above cited newspaper article also noticed that Mashhadi Jews, when gathering together in a private house or even a basement for saying collective prayers, had a habit of leaving their wives outside; these wives, by encircling the house, thus contrived to prevent Moslems from seeing what was going on inside.[289] Mashhadi Jews would not work on Saturdays, leaving their shops in the charge of teenager servants, who, in turn, not willing to work on Sabbath days either, raised enormously the prices of the goods offered for sale.[290]

Naimark's report gives us the names of the persons who headed the community at the time he visited Marv in 1886: Moshe Cohen, Amin (Benyamin) Kurtovani, and Yakov the Shoikhet (cattle

---

[287] TsGHAU, f. 1, op. 17, d. 922, p. 17; Voskhod, 1902. At the same time, Djedids in the Transcaspian oblast went to mosques regularly. Vaisenberg, 1916, p. 82.
[288] Vaisenberg, 1916, p. 82.
[289] Ibid.
[290] Ibid.

slaughterer), a former Mashhadi synagogue warden.[291] Another Jewish traveler, Nahum Levi Isaac Abreq, found it worth mentioning that the community had no rabbi. As to the shoikhet, he was semiskilled.[292] Though seemingly referring to the shoikhet's professionalism, this criticism could probably mean only that the tradition of cattle-slaughtering the local shoikhet stuck to, disagreed with the Hasid traveler's views on this issue. As a matter of fact, the slaughtering scheme practiced by Ashkenazi Misnagdim was different from the one adopted by Ashkenazi Hasidim, each of them being unlike the shekhita of Sefardic Jews. The conflict between the advocates of the Sephardic way of shekhita and the followers of the Hasidic method of ritual cattle slaughtering resulted at the end of the 19th and the beginning of the 20th century in acute clashes within the Bukharan Jewish community of Central Asia.[293] Be that as it may, the shekhita standards in Marv must have improved in the late 1890s, when Herati cattle slaughterers Aaron Suleimanov and Rakhman Iazgel Yusufov settled there. The two were living in Marv until the mass expulsion of Herati Jews from the Transcaspian oblast in 1910-1911.[294] At the time mentioned, Marv Djedids had Nathan Kaziyev as their leader, with Babadjan Suleimanov and Nathaniel Ashurov being his assistants.[295] The community had, to all appearance, developed well-arranged self-governance mechanisms by then.

Iosif, a son of the chief Herat rabbi Mattatia Gordzhi, stopped in Marv on his way to Eretz Israel via Russia in 1903. Iosif Gordzhi (1869-1937) yielded to the earnest requests made to him by two rich representatives of the Herati Jewish community of Marv, Nathan Kozi and Djura-bai Iglanov (of whom also see above), to

---

[291] Naimark, 1889, p. 69.
[292] Abreq, 1887, p. 2.
[293] Kaganovich, Attitude, 2003, pp. 123-124.
[294] TsGHAU, f. 1, op. 17, d. 922, pp. 108-109.
[295] Ibid, p. 46.

stay in Marv permanently and fill the position of the town rabbi.[296] Until then, according to the Russian administration, it was his uncle Shmuel Shalomayev, a city resident since 1872, i.e. the time before the Russian invasion, who had been the town rabbi.[297] This man, named in Hebrew sources Shmuel Bar Shlema Gordzhi, also served the community as shoikhet and melamed.[298] As it seems, Iosif Gordzhi, to say nothing of his predecessor, was not enjoying full recognition as an authoritative rabbi by his rabbi colleagues; this is evidenced by the fact that he was not entitled the lawful right to divorce married couples, which right would normally be given to experts in the rabbinical law by prominent rabbis. It was that limitation of legal power that made divorcing Mashhadi Jews from Marv appeal to the chief rabbi of Bukhara; Aga-Djan, son of Suleiman, and Ferdji Ala, for instance, made such appeals in 1905 and 1909, respectively.[299] After the already mentioned expulsion of 1910-1911, Iosif Gordzhi left for Jerusalem to join his father, who had settled there by that time. Shmuel Gordzhi returned to Herat, although he subsequently used to come to the Transcaspian oblast on trading business. Russian law allowed foreign Jews to visit the

---

[296] Ieshua-Raz, 1992, pp. 242, 471-473.
[297] TsGHAU, f. 1, op. 17, d. 922, p. 46.
[298] Ieshua-Raz, 1992, pp. 471-473.
[299] Rabin, 1992, pp. 270, 278. The Bukharan rabbi still would divorce married couples living in Marv, after the rabbi Josef Gordzhi's departure from the town. He continued to arrange divorces of Jews from Marv even later, under the Soviet regime. Thus, in 1923 he divorced a Mashhadi Jew Rahamim Hadji, son of Itskhak Yezdi. Ibid, pp. 292, 310. From the father's second name – Yezdi – one can conclude that the family came from Yezd; the son's second name – Hadji – is indicative of the pilgrimage to Mecca he probably did. The same document told of another Marv Jew of non-Ashkenazi origin, who divorced during the same year, Elkhanan, son of Itskhak; no indication being made of his Djedid roots, though. A certain Mahamed Hussein, son of Habib-Allah, a Mashhadi Jew, was divorced by the Bukharan rabbi in 1927. Ibid, p. 317. It goes without saying that all divorcees, no matter if from Marv or from other places, whom the Bukharan rabbi divorced, registered their new, unmarried status at local civil registration offices, their divorce being otherwise illegal. It is probable also that Herati Jews, in the absence of their own rabbi, applied, or at any rate had to apply, to the Bukharan rabbi for getting divorced. One such case is known to have been in 1915. Ibid, p. 335.

country, provided that their stays in Russia lasted less than a month and a half. It was on one of his visits to Marv in 1912-1913 when Vaisenberg, who tells of him as of a rabbi, met him there.[300] Shmuel, as one may suppose, appeared in Marv to finish up the business affairs he had in town. He left for Jerusalem permanently soon thereafter.[301]

The first synagogue (or beth-midrash, as another source calls it)[302] known to have been in Marv was opened by Herati and Mashhadi Djedids prior to the invasion of Turkmenia in 1871. In 1894 it was closed for a period by Russian authorities,[303] but it must have been re-opened shortly after, for there is a statistical report published in 1900 that reported three synagogues constructed of brick found in Marv,[304] supposedly belonging to Mashhadi, Herati and Bukharan Jews. The same source mentioned another synagogue constructed in stone in Iolatan.[305] Djedids had a synagogue in Pende in the 1890s.[306] It is most probable that the Djedid synagogue in Serakhs, seen by Naimark in 1886,[307] still existed in the last decade of the 19th century, as well as the synagogue opened by Takhta-Bazar Djedid residents in the late 1880s.[308]

A synagogue in Marv, apparently the one that belonged to Mashhadi Djedids, was closed in 1902 by the order of the uezd administrator F.A. Mikhailov, on the grounds that monetary aid

---

[300] Vaisenberg, 1916, p. 82.
[301] Fuzailov, Rabbis, 1995, p. 206.
[302] Naimark, 1889, pp. 68-69. For its existence in the middle 1880s see: Tikhomirov, 1960, p. 165.
[303] Leivi, 1930, p. 18; Vaisenberg, 1912, p. 404.
[304] Obzor, 1902, p. 138.
[305] Ibid.
[306] Kasheni, 1981, p. 280.
[307] Naimark, 1889, p. 75. Naimark reported of a visitation of Ashkenazi Jews – soldiers in the Russian army – made to that synagogue. They were reported to turn to the eastern wall while saying prayers, much to the astonishment of Mashhadi Jews, who used to turn westward at prayer.
[308] TsGHAU, f. 1, op. 13, d. 676, p. 27a.; Hazioni, 1913, pp. 43-44.

was sent to Jerusalem by the Marv community.[309] Mashhadi Jews used to contribute money to Jewish inhabitants of Eretz Israel profusely, either on their frequent visits to Palestine, or by sending it with messengers[310] an activity always frowned upon by the Russian authorities, whether in Central Asia or in the western provinces of the Empire,[311] with the plausible reason that those donations were not only wasting down the monetary resources of Russian Jews, but also subsidizing the Ottoman Empire, the arch-enemy of Russians. That Mashhadi synagogue was opened again, possibly with the permission of the Military governor E.K. Ussakovskii who favored Jews. It closed down finally no sooner than in 1907, as Aba Lev was informed.[312] It must have been this big and handsome synagogue, though closed, that impressed Vaisenberg so much.[313] An official report dated 1910 mentioned of two synagogues in Marv and one in Tejen.[314] No information about synagogues in Iolatan, Serakhs and Takhta-Bazar is available otherwise. It is not improbable that the synagogues were forcibly closed. On the other hand, Djedids might have kept them from the oversight of the authorities. In places, where they had no synagogues, Djedids would apparently congregate for prayer

---

[309] Voskhod, 1902. About the donations made by Marv Djedids see: Account, 1893, p. 267.
[310] Abreq, 1887, p. 2; Hazioni, 1913, p. 44; Ieshua-Raz, 1992, pp. 125, 146, 258-262; Nissimi, 2003, p. 83.
[311] For instance, an envoy from Jerusalem, Aharon Alcolay by name, who collected money for the needs of his community, was arrested in Zhitomir (today Ukraine) in 1836. As soon as the police investigation of his "crime" was finished, which took more than a year, he was deported out of the country. Central Archive of Jewish History in Jerusalem, f. HM2/8925.2, pp. 5a-6a, 36, 93. Russian authorities negatively regarded the envoys sent from Jerusalem, among them Isaak Yankel Khislavitskii, a Rabbi of the Ashkenazi community of Jerusalem sent in 1869 to Tobolsk, and Ieshua ben David Mizrahi, a rabbi of Iranian and Caucasian Jews in Jerusalem, who was sent to Kovno (now Kaunas) in 1873. Ibid, HM2/7979, pp. 3-5; HM2/8002.6, pp. 1-8. HM2/7979, pp. 3-5; HM2/8002.6, pp. 1-8.
[312] Lev, 1913
[313] Vaisenberg, 1912, p. 404; Vaisenberg, 1916, p. 82.
[314] Obzor, 1913, p. 336.

services and holiday celebrations in private homes.

Those Mashhadi Djedids who still resided in the Transcaspian oblast after the 1910 expulsion seemingly redoubled their efforts to conceal their devotion to the Jewish tradition. Mashhadi Djedids would not participate in the religious practices of Bukharan Jews and publicly abstained from associating with them, fearing the risk of being expelled. These fears provide an explanation for the difficulties the Bukharan Jews of Russian citizenship had in gathering minyan after the forced migration of the Bukharan Jews of Bukharan citizenship took place in 1911.[315] It is most likely that Mashhadi Djedids avoided public contacts with those Herati Jews still remaining in the province at the time as well.

The percentage of Djedids who visited Eretz Israel was higher compared with that of other Iranian Jewish communities. On those visits, they made lavish donations to Jewish religious foundations in the Holy Land in order to "expiate the sin" of converting into Islam. Some Djedids stayed in Jerusalem permanently, living, along with the city's Bukharan Jews, in a separate quarter the latter had since the early 1890s.[316] One of those, a certain mulla Khanuka Ben Aga Dzhoni Shemesh, was known to be born in Marv in 1863 and set out for Jerusalem in 1891.[317] It may be mentioned as a curious fact that Jews of Mashhadi origin remain renown for their special piety and yearning for Israel among their Iranian coreligionists even today.[318]

Obviously enough, Djedids already had small heders by the time the Russians invaded Turkmenia. Despite the fact that they forwarded a petition to the Military governor of the Transcaspian oblast A.V. Komarov, asking for his permission to open a Jewish

---

[315] Bachaev, 1990, pp. 87-88.
[316] Letters from Jerusalem, 1896; Verman, 1991, pp. 70-75; Fuzailov, From Bukhara to Jerusalem, 1995, p. 197.
[317] Ieshua-Raz, 1992, p. 474.
[318] A work by a rabbi Michael Reichel confirms this. Reichel, 2004, pp. 90-94.

religious school in Marv, such permission officially granted in 1884,[319] we may assume that the issue of the official document was a mere act to legalize the already existing school. By 1900, there were two two-year Jewish schools in Marv, one for Bukharan Jews (opened in 1886), and the other one for Herati Jews. The Herati Jews' school had 45 pupils; religious subjects and Hebrew were taught there.[320] After graduation from the schools, pupils, to the knowledge of the local administration, continued their education in Samarkand and Bukhara.[321] In 1901, the schools were put by an administrative decree under the supervision of Ministry of Education, being transformed into so-called Russian native schools. The new status meant the obligation of teaching pupils the Russian language, along with Hebrew; non-compliance with this requirement might have entailed closure of the school.[322] Presumably, the requirement was met. As Ben-Zion Ieshua-Raz reported, boys and girls sat in the same class-room, having a class in the Herati Jews' school.[323]

Besides that school, old traditional heders still existed in Marv in the beginning of the 20th century, as well as in the other places in Turkmenia where Djedids resided. In heders, children, in the main, memorized prayers, but were not taught to read. Existence of those heders offers a possible explanation for the fact that by 1920 the literacy rate among "native Jewish" males in Turkmenia, i.e. almost totally Djedids, was 27.3%.[324] This figure implied literacy in any language including Hebrew – the predominant language of teaching among Turkmenian Djedids. Of all nationalities living in Turkmenia they were in the third place by percentage of literate

---

[319] Obzor, 1902, pp. 245, 268.
[320] Ibid.
[321] Ibid.
[322] Ibid. For the "Russian native schools" in Turkestanskii krai see: Kaganovich, Education, 2003, pp. 207-209.
[323] Ieshua-Raz, 1992, p. 129.
[324] Statistical yearbook, 1924, p. 66.

males, after Russians (literacy rate 67.7%) and Armenians (50.8%), having higher literacy index than Iranians (14.3%), Uzbeks (9.1%), Kazakhs (2.4%), Turkmen (1.1%) and other Turkic nationalities.[325] According to the male literacy rate statistics gathered in the Samarkand and Syrdaria oblasts, Herati and Mashhadi Jews in Turkmenian settlements had a somewhat higher percentage of literate males, compared to the other "native Jews" of the Samarkand and Syrdaria oblasts, i.e. Bukharan Jews. Samarkand was an important cultural center of the region in general and the metropolis of Bukharan Jews of Central Asia in particular, where 7,400 (at least one third from all this ethnos) of them were living by 1920; 25.2% of Jewish residents were literate, with still lower rates in other parts of the two oblasts. It was only in Tashkent that the literacy rate of Bukharan Jews was much higher and came to 43.8%.[326] Herati and Mashhadi Jews, like any other people living in the region, showed lesser interest in teaching girls. Female literacy index among Herati and Mashhadi Jews in Turkmenia was 3.1%, lower than that of the local Russians, Armenians and Iranians, though higher than the literacy rate of any of the Turkic nationalities. It exceeded the analogous indices of the Bukharan Jewish females of the Samarkand oblast, but was significantly inferior to the literacy rates that females of the same ethnic group had in the Syrdaria oblast, namely 18.5%.[327] Such a difference can be explained by taking into account the cultural influence the Bukharan Jews were exposed to in Tashkent.

While the school owned by the Jews of Bukharan citizenship residing in Marv closed down after their mass expulsion in January 1911,[328] the Herati Jews' school continued its work and survived the October revolution in 1917.[329] Its program in the 1920s

---
[325] Ibid.
[326] Ibid.
[327] Ibid.
[328] Kaganovich, 2003, p. 159.
[329] V Turkestane, 1921.

undoubtedly corresponded with that of any other Soviet school. Using Hebrew as teaching language was out of the question (since all efforts to learn and teach Hebrew were actively opposed by the Jewish Bureau of the Communist Party), so it was replaced by the Gilaki dialect of Persian. In the beginning of the 1930s the Soviet authorities made Russian the only language of teaching permitted in the Jewish school of Marv,[330] coming thus back to the principles of russification of Central Asia fostered in former days by the Tsarist government.

Alongside with this public school in Marv, and also in Iolatan and probably in Bairam-Ali up to 1940-1950, there were clandestine traditional heders. Children attended them after lessons in the comprehensive schools. In these cities communities of Herati and Mashhadi Jews continued to exist. Up to 1930 they had synagogues. The synagogue in Iolatan existed longer than the other ones. It was closed in 1939 during the purge of "unreliable elements" discussed above.[331]

In the late 1920s it had a theatre company playing in the Gilaki dialect of Persian, in the spirit of the communist decrees stimulating the formation of national theatres.[332] The company, it seems, was active until the beginning of the 1930s, when the mass migration of Mashhadi and Herati Jews from Central Asia began.

---

[330] Kupovetskii, 1992, p. 62.
[331] Interview with Iehuda Kohen, May 12, 2006 and Arkadii Betsalel, May 10, 2006 (from the author's own archive).
[332] Ibid.

Summary

In summation, Mashhadi Jews, including their Herati offshoot, were preserved in Turkmenia as a marginal group and lived there for as long as one hundred and fifty years. This group reached its fullest flower during the first decade of the 20th century, when its ties with the Jewish world strengthened and its identity was highly emphasized. Later on, this group suffered a drastic decrease in numbers, due to the policy of the Russian government to banish foreign Jews out of the Russian territory. After a short-term upturn in 1917-1920 the Djedid communities of Turkmenia found themselves in a lasting economic, social and spiritual crisis. Loss of ethnic identity was a common problem, when the last Mashhadi and Herati Jews were leaving Turkmenia in the 1990s (nearly all who remained).

As to the Mashhadi and Herati Jews who lived outside of Russia (later the USSR), the presence of Djedid colonies in Turkmenia and the possibility to trade there, despite the fact that their rights were restricted by the Tsarist authorities, were an important factor of economic prosperity for their communities in Iran and Afghanistan. It allowed Jews, mainly those living in the biggest communities of Mashhad and Herat, to focus to a greater degree on their religious life and to invest more in educational pursuits. However, the economic reforms that came about in the USSR in the late 1920s to the early 1930s and the border closing in the middle of the 1930s deprived Mashhadi and Herati Jews of their main source of revenue. Their living in Iran and Afghanistan ceased to be economically justified, unlike in the times when the practice of unobstructed trade with Russia provided an economic mechanism to support their mother communities, primarily the ones in Mashhad and Herat.

Illustration 2: Advertisements. *Konopka S.P., Turkestanskii krai*, Tashkent, 1912, p. 20

Illustration 3: Turkmens. B. Golender, Okno v proshloe, Tashkent, 2002, p. 236

Bibliography

Abezguz, 1904
Абезгуз М.М., Тегеранские евреи, глава XVII, *Книжки Восхода*, №5, 1904, с. 84-110.

Abreq, 1887
נ.ל.י. אברק, היהודים באזיה התיכונה, היום, 14.07.1887, גל'
154, עמ' 2-4.

Account, 1893
חשבון ועד החברה לתמיכת בני ישראל עובדי אדמה ובעלי
מלאכה בסוריה ובארץ הקדוש בשנים 1890-1892, אודסה, 1893.

Adler, Jews in Many Lands, 1905
Adler E.N., *Jews in Many Lands*, Philadelphia, 1905.
Adler, The Jews of Bokhara, 1905
Adler E.N., The Jews of Bokhara, *The Jewish chronicle*, 27.01.1905, p. 28.

Aini, 1960
Айни С., *Воспоминания*, Москва-Ленинград, 1960.

Aitakov, 1929
Айтаков Н., *Пять лет Туркмении*, Ашхабад, 1929.

Alikhanov, 1883
Алиханов М., *Мервский оазис и дороги ведущие к нему*, С. Петербург, 1883.

Amitin-Shapiro, 1933

Амитин-Шапиро З.Л., *Очерки социалистического строительства среди среднеазиатских евреев*, Ташкент, 1933.

Asherov, 1977
ש. אשרוב, <u>מסמרקנד עד פתח-תקוה</u>, תל-אביב, 1977

Ataev, 1971
Атаев Х., Торговля туркменов Ирана с Россией, *Известия Академии наук Туркменской ССР* (общественные науки), №6, 1971, с. 13-19.

Ataev, 1989
Атаев Х., *Политические и торговые отношения северо-восточного Ирана и России в начале 20 века*, Ашхабад, 1989.

Babakhodzhaev, 1965
Бабаходжаев М.А. *Русско-афганские торгово-экономические отношения во второй половине XVIII - начале XX в*, Ташкент, 1965.

Babakhodzhaev, 1975
Бабаходжаев М.А., *Очерки социально-экономической и политической истории Афганистана (конец XIX века)*, Ташкент, 1975.

Bachaev, 1990
מ.ח. בצ'איב (מוחיב), <u>בתוך "שק האבן"</u>, ירושלים, 1990

Bekmakhanova, 1986
Бекмаханова Н.Е., *Формирование многонационального населения Казахстана и Северной Киргизии в эпоху капитализма*, Москва, 1986.

Benari, 1910
Бенари А., Джедиды, *Туркестанский курьер*, №195, 29.08.1910, с. 2.

Benjamin, 1859
Benjamin I.J., *Eight years in Asia and Africa*, Hanover, 1859.

Ben-Zvi, 1966
י. בן-צבי , עלילות-דם וגזירות-שמד במשהד בסלמס ונהיראת
במאה הי"ט, מחקרים ומקורות, ירושלים, 1966, עמ' 319-334.

Berlin, 1911
Берлин И., Джедиды, *Еврейская энциклопедия*, том 7, 1911, с. 153-154.

Blaramberg, 1853
Бларамберг И.Ф., *Статистическое обозрение Персии, составленное подполковником И.Ф. Бларамбергом в 1841 г.*, С. Петербург, 1853.

Budushchnost', 1902
Будущность, 1902, №22, с. 430.
Budushchnost, 1902
Будущность, 1902, №48, с. 952.

Burnes, 1839
Burnes A., *Travels into Bokhara*, vol. 1-3, London, 1839.

Census, 1926
Всесоюзная перепись населения 1926 года, том 16, Туркменская СССР, Москва, 1928.
Census, 1939
Distribution of the Jewish Population of the USSR 1939, ed. M. Altshuler, Jerusalem, 1993.

Conolly, 1834
Conolly A., *Journey to the North India, Overland from England through Russia, Persia and Afganistan*, London, vol. 1-2, 1834.

Curzon, 1892
Curzon G., *Persia and the Persian Question*, vol. 1-2, London, 1892.

Dakhtaev, 1992
Дахтаев Ю.И., *О бухарских евреях*, Душанбе, 1992.

Dilmanian, 1997
Dilmanian Y., *History of the Jews of Mashad, 1746-1946, AD: from their entrance to Mashad at the time of Nader Shah Afshar until their migration from Mashad to Tehran*, ?, 1997.

Dmitriev-Mamonov, 1912
Дмитриев-Мамонов А.И., *Путеводитель по Туркестану и Средне-Азиатской железной дороге*, С. Петербург, 1912.

Dobson, 1890
G. Dobson, *Russia's Railway advance into Central Asia*, London, 1890.

Entner, 1965
Entner M., Russo-Persian Commercial Relations, 1828-1914, *University of Florida Monographs, Social Sciences*, no. 28, Gainesville, 1965.

Evrei v Persii, 1899
Евреи в Персии, *Восход*, №52, 25.11.1899, с. 1653-1655.

Evreiskaia tribuna, 1922
Еврейская трибуна (Paris), №110, 02.02.1922, с. 7.

Evreiskoe obozrenie, 1910
Еврейское обозрение, №9, 22.07.1910, с. 19.

Expulsion from Bukhara, 1911
הגרוש מבוכארה, האור, 25.01.1911, גל' 83 (258), עמ' 2

Expulsion of the Bukharan Jews, 1911
גרוש היהודים הבוכרים, החרות, 20.01.1911, גל' 39, עמ' 3

Expulsion of Jews, 1910
גרוש יהודים מחבל הכספי, האור, 11.08.1910, גל' 131, עמ' 3

The Famine in Persia, 1872.
הרעב בפרס, הכרמל, 29.03.1872, עמ' 312

Fedorov, 1913
Фёдоров Г.М., Моя служба в Туркестанском крае, *Исторический вестник*, №12, 1913, с. 860-893.

Ferrier, 1857
Ferrier J.P., *Caravan journeys and wanderings in Persia, Afghanistan, Turkistan and Beloochistan: with historical notices of the countries lying between Russia and India*, London, 1857 (reprint, Westmead, 1971).

Fischel, 1936
ו.י. פישל, קהלת האנוסים בפרס, ציון, 1936, גל' 1, עמ' -79
49.

Fischel, 1945

Fischel W., The Jews of Central Asia (Khorasan) in Medieval Hebrew and Islamic Literature, *Historia Judaica* 7, 1945, p. 29-50.

Fischel, 1949

Fischel W.J., Secret Jews of Persia: A Century-Old Marrano Community in Asia, *Commentary*, vol. VII, January 1949 - June 1949, pp. 28-33.

Fischel, 1964

Fischel W.J., The Leaders of the Jews of Bokhara, *Jewish Leaders*, ed. L. Jung, Jerusalem, 1964, pp. 535-547.

Fischel, 1982

Fischel W.J., The Jews in Medieval Iran from the 16th to the 18th Centuries: Political, Economical and Communal Aspects, *Irano-Judaica*, 1982, pp. 285-286.

Forbes, 1940

Forbes R., *Russian Road to India by Kabul and Samarkand*, London, 1940.

Forster, 1798

Forster G. A., *Journey from Bengal to England through the North of India, Afghanistan and Persia into Russia*, 2 vols., London, 1798.

Fox, 1925

Fox R., *People of the Steppes*, Boston and New York, 1925.

Fraser, 1984

Fraser J. B., *Narrative of a journey into Khorasan in the years 1821 and 1822*, London, 1825 (reprint, Delhi, 1984).

Fuzailov, Rabbis, 1995

ג. פוזיילוב, חכמיהם של יהודי פרס ואפגניסטאן, ירושלים, 1995.

Fuzailov, From Bukhara to Jerusalem, 1995
ג. פוזיילוב, <u>מבוכארה לירושלים</u>, ירושלים, 1995

Gordzhi, 1970
מ. גורד"י, קורות זמנים לרב מתתיה גורד"י מאפגניסטאן (עורך
ראובן קשאני), <u>שבט ועם</u>, סידרה שניה, א' (ו'), 1970, עמ' 136 - 169.

Harel, 1983
מ. הראל (בבאיוף), <u>נחלת יעקב</u>, תל-אביב, 1983

Hazioni, 1913
Hazioni, На далёкой окраине (письмо из Тахта-Базара), *Рассвет*, №50, 13.12.1913, с. 43-44.

The Jews in Merv, 1899
The Jews in Merv, *Jewish Chronicle*, 12.05.1899, p. 17.

Ian, 1989
Ян В.Г., *Собрание сочинений в 4 томах*, Москва, 1989.

Iavorskiy, 1889
Яворский И.Л., *Опыт медицинской и географической статистики Туркестана*, часть 1, С. Петербург, 1889.

Idelzon, 1920
א.צ. אידלזון, יהודי בוכרא, <u>מזרח ומערב</u>, תר"פ, חוברת א,
כרך ראשון, 1920, עמ' 317-326.

Ieshua-Raz, 1992
ב.-צ. יהושע-רז, <u>מנידחי ישראל באפגניסטאן לאנוסי משהד
באיראן</u>, ירושלים, 1992.

Ivanov, 1952
Иванов М.С., *Очерк истории Ирана*, 1952.

Ivanov, 1954
Иванов П.П., *Хозяйство джуйбарских шейхов*, Москва-Ленинград, 1954.

Iz Herata, 1880
[Из Герата], *Рассвет*, №6, 07.02.1880, с. 217.

Jews in Afghanistan, 1878
היהודים באפגאניסטאן , הצפירה , 17.02.1878 , גל ' 48 , עמ' 379.

Kabuzan, 1996
Кабузан В.М., *Эмиграция и резмиграция в России в XVIII – начале XX века*, Москва, 1998.

Kaganovich, 1995
Каганович А.Б., О евреях-мусульманах, проживающих в Туркестанском крае, *Евреи в Средней Азии, Труды по иудаике Петербургского еврейского университета*, Выпуск 4, 1995, с. 116-132.

Kaganovich, 1997
Kaganovich A., The Legal and Political Situation of the Muslim Jews in Russian Turkestan 1865-1917, *Shvut*, no. 6 (22), 1997, pp. 57-78.

Kaganovich, Education, 2003
Kaganovich A., The Education of Bukharan Jews in Turkestan province 1865-1917, *Irano-Judaica*, vol. V, 2003, pp. 202-213.

Kaganovich, Attitude, 2003

Kaganovich A., *The Attitude of the Czarist Administration to the Bukharan Jews and Their Legal Status in Turkestan in the Years 1867 - 1917*, Doctoral dissertation, submitted to the Senate of the Hebrew University, Jerusalem, 2003.

Kalontarov, 1963
[Калонтаров Л.Н], Среднеазиатские евреи, *Народы Средней Азии и Казахстана*, том 2, 1963, с. 610-630.

Kasheni, 1981
ר' קשאני, מסעות הרב מולה מתתיה גרג׳י מאפגניסטן לארץ ישראל בתרנ״ו- 1896 ובתרס״ח1908-, שבט ועם, סדרה שניה, ד. (ט'), 1981, עמ' 263-289.

Kazembeyki, 2003
Kazembeyki M.A., *Society, Politics and Economics in Mazandaran, Iran, 1848-1914*, London, 2003.

Khalfin, 1965
Халфин Н.А., *Присоединение Средней Азии к России (60-90-е годы 19 века)*, Москва, 1965.

Khanykov, 1973
Ханыков Н., *Экспедиция в Хорасан (1858-1859)*, Москва, 1973.

Khoroshkhin, 1876
Хорошхин А.П., Заметка о закете в Бухарском ханстве, в книге: Хорошхин А.П., *Сборник статей, касающихся до Туркестанского края*, С. Петербург, 1876, с. 294-300.

Kokand Stock Exchange Committee, 1912

Кокандский биржевой комитет 1912 г., Коканд, 1913.
Kokand Stock Exchange Committee, 1913
Кокандский биржевой комитет 1913 г., Коканд, 1914.

Konopka, 1912
Конопка С.Р., *Туркестанский край*, Ташкент, 1912.

Koplik, 2003
Koplik S., The Demise of Afghanistan's Jewish Community and the Soviet Refugee Crisis (1932-1936), *Iranian Studies*, volume 36, no. 3, 2003, pp. 353-379.

Kostyrchenko, 2001
Костырченко Г.В., *Тайная политика Сталина*, Москва, 2001.

Kupovetskii, 1992
Куповецкий М.С., Евреи из Мешхеда и Герата в Средней Азии, *Этнографическое обозрение*, №5, 1992, с. 54-64.

Kuznetsova, 1980
Кузнецова Н.А., Об участии немусульман в торговле Ирана, *Ближний и средний Восток. Товарно-денежные отношения при феодализме*, Москва, 1980, с. 117-127.

Kuznetsova, 1983
Кузнецова Н.А., *Иран в первой половине XIX века*, Москва, 1983.

Lansdell, 1885
Lansdell H.D., *Russian Central Asia*, vol. 1-2, Boston, 1885.

Laws on conditions, 1899

Законы о состояниях, издание 1899, *Свод законов Российской империи,* том IX, Москва, 1910.

Leivi, 1930
Лейви Д., Положение евреев при Куропаткине, *Туркменоведение,* №11, 1930, с. 17-18.

Lessar, 1884
Лессар П.М., Заметки о Закаспийском крае и соседних странах, *Записки Кавказского отделения императорского РГО,* книга 13, 1884, с. 161-211.
Lessar, Turkmenistan, 1884
Лессар П.М., Юго-Западная Туркмения 1884 г., *Сборник географических и статистических материалов по Азии,* выпуск 13, С. Петербург, 1884 , с. 1-137.

Letters from Jerusalem, 1896
היל"ל בן שכ"ר, מכתבים מירושלים, <u>המגיד</u>, 30.04.1896, גל'
17, עמ' 137-138.

Lev, 1913
א. לעוו, האנוסים בבוכארה, <u>הצפירה</u>, גל' 138 , 20.06.1913,
עמ' 3.

Levene, 1932
Levene M., The Marranos of Persia, *The Jewish Chronicle,* 08.01.1932, p. 16.

Levy, 1987
ע. לוי, <u>יהודי משהד</u>, ירושלים, תשמ"ז
Levy, 1980

ע. לוי, עדויות ותעודות לתולדות יהודי משהד, <u>פעמים</u>, 1980, גל' 6, עמ' 57-73.

List of denotation, 1890
<u>חשבון נדבות</u>, 1890, ירושלים.

Mannanov, 1962
Маннанов Б., Из истории русско-иранских торгово-экономических отношений через Туркестан (конец XIX – начало XX века), *Общественные науки в Узбекистане*, №9, 1962, с. 46-53.

Meyendorf, 1826
G. de Meyendorff, *Voyage d'Orenburg a Boukhara, fait en 1820*, Paris, 1826.

Miller, 1909
Миллер Г.П., Отрывки из воспоминаний, *Исторический вестник*, том 118, 1909, с. 887-891.

Mishal, 1981
י. מישאל, <u>בין אפגניסתאן לארץ-ישראל</u>, ירושלים, תשמ"א.

Moreen, 1986
Moreen V.B., The problems of Conversion among Iranian Jews in the Seventeenth and Eighteenth Centuries, *Iranian Studies*, vol. 19, no. 3-4, 1986, pp. 215-228.

Motrevich and Proshchenok, 1997
V. Motrevich and T. Proshchenok, Foreign Citizens of Jewish Origin in the USSR, according to the 1937 Census, *Jews in Eastern Europe*, no. 1 (32), 1997, pp. 27-33.

Naimark, 1889

א. נאיימרק, ארץ הקדם, <u>האסיף</u>, 1889, עמ' 39 - 75

Netzer, 1985

א. נצר, <u>אוצר כתבי היד של יהודי פרס במכון בן-צבי</u>, ירושלים, 1985.

Netzer, 1990

א. נצר, קורות אנוסי משהד לפי יעקב דילמאניאן, <u>פעמים</u>, 1990, גל' 42, עמ' 127 - 156

Nissimi, 2003

Nissimi H., Memory, Community, and the Mashhadi Jews during the Underground Period, *Jewish Social Studies*, vol. 9 (3), 2003, pp. 76-106.

Novyi Voskhod, 1910

Новый Восход, №17, 22.07.1910, с. 12

Obzor, 1893

Обзор Закаспийской области за 1892, Асхабад, 1893.

Obzor, 1900

Обзор Закаспийской области за 1898, Асхабад, 1900.

Obzor, 1902

Обзор Закаспийской области за 1900, Асхабад, 1902.

Obzor, 1913

Обзор Закаспийской области за 1910 г., Асхабад, 1913.

Obzor, 1915

Обзор Закаспийской области за 1911, Асхабад, 1915.

O'Donovan, 1882.

O'Donovan E., *The Merv*, vol. 1-2, London, 1882.

News from borders of Israel, 1862
חדשות בגבול ישראל, המליץ, 26.04.1862, גל' 29, עמ' 457-451.

Patai, 1946
ר' פטאי, החנוך העברי בעדת האנוסים במשהד, עדות, שנה א, כרך א, תש"ו, עמ' 213-226.

Patai, 1997
Patai R., *Jadid al-Islam*, Detroit, 1997.

Pilosof-Pinkhasof, 1970
ע. פלוסוף-פינחסוף, תיאורי עמנואל, תל-אביב, 1970.

Pinkhasi, 1978
י. פינחסי, עשרה סיפורי - עם מבוכארה, ירושלים, 1978.

Rivlin, 1887
ש.מ. ריבלין, מערב, היום, 17.03.1887, גל' 63, עמ' 1-2.

Polian, 2001
Полян П., *Не по своей воле: История и география принудительных миграций в СССР*, Москва, 2001.

Population of Russia, 2000
Население России в XX веке: Исторические очерки (редактор Ю.А. Поляков), том 1, Москва, 2000.

Prilozhenie, 1916
Приложение к обзору Закаспийской области за 1911, 1913, 1914, Асхабад, 1916,

Rabin, 1989

י. הכהן רבין, זרח כוכב מיעקב, ירושלים, 1989

Rabin, 1992
י' רבין, עטרת חזקיה, ירושלים, 1992

Rakhamim, 1911
רחמים, 03.06.1911, גל' 37, עמ' 2

Rassvet, 1910, no. 29
Рассвет, №29, 18.07.1910, с. 17-18.
Rassvet, 1910, no. 46
Рассвет, №46, 14.11.1910, с. 20.
Rassvet, 1910, no. 50
Рассвет, №50, 12.12.1910, с. 54-55.

Rediger, 1999
Редигер А.Ф., *История моей жизни*, том 1-2, Москва, 1999.

Reichel, 2004
Reichel M., *Persian American Jewry at a crossroads: will the tradititions continue*, New-York, 2004.

Rivlin, 1888
שמ"ר בן פא"ר (ש.מ. ריבלין), מכתבים מבוכארה, המליץ, 29.0.9.1888, גל' 209, עמ' 3095-3098.

Samuel, 1840
Samuel J., *An Appeal on Behalf of the Jews scattered in India, Persia, and Arabia*, London, 1840.

Sbornik svedeniy, 1885

Сборник сведений о Средней Азии и русском Туркестане, Ташкент, 1885.

Sevast'ianov, 1929
Севастьянов И., *Странички прошлого Туркмении и сопредельных стран с нею*, Ашхабад, 1929.

Slousch, 1909
Slousch N., Les Juifs à Boukhara, *Revue du Monde musulman*, no. 7, 1909, pp. 402-413.

Statistical yearbook, 1914
Статистический ежегодник на 1914, С. Петербург, 1914.
Statistical yearbook, 1924
Статистический ежегодник 1917-1923, том 1, часть 3, Ташкент, 1924.

Stewart, 1977
Stewart C.E., The Country of the Tekke Turkomans, *The Country of the Turkomans*, London, 1977, pp. 124-172.

Sukhareva, 1966
Сухарева О.А., *Бухара 19 - начала 20 века*, Москва, 1966.

Suleimani, 1966
Пайрав Сулеймани, Пайрав Сулеймани о себе, *Советские писатели*, том 3, Москва, 1966, с. 530-532.

Svet, 1907
Свет (Санкт-Петербург), №88, 1907, с. 3.

Telegram from Merv, 1910

[Телеграмма из Мерва], *Новый Восход*, №33, 11.11.1910, с. 19.

Tikhomirov, 1960
Тихомиров М.Н., *Присоединение Мерва к России*, Москва, 1960.

Tolmas, 2000
Tolmas Ch., *Antroponymy of Bukharan Jews*, Doctoral dissertation, submitted to the Senate of the Hebrew University, Jerusalem, 2001.

Trislov, 1902
Трислов, К истории вопроса о праве жительства в Закаспийской области туземных евреев, *Асхабад*, №317, 13.11.1902, с. 1-2; №318, 14.11.1902, с. 2.

Tsadik, 2005
ד. צדיק, היהודים בכלכלה המדינה, איראן, עמ' 41-54

Turkestanskie vedomosti, 1884
Туркестанские ведомости, №14, 1884, с. 67.
Turkestanskie vedomosti, 1905
Туркестанские ведомости, №166, 1905, с. 866.

Turkmenistan, 1996
Туркменистан, *Краткая еврейская энциклопедия*, том 8, Иерусалим, 1996, с. 1103-1106.

Yusupov, 1993
Юсупов Ф., Иранцы, *Так это было*, том 1, Москва, 1993, с. 87-92.

V Turkestane, 1921
В Туркестане, *Жизнь национальностей*, №20, 03.10.1921, с. 3.

Vaisenberg, 1912
Вайсенберг С.А., Евреи в Туркестане, *Еврейская старина*, том 5, 1912, с. 390-405.

Vaisenberg, 1916
Вайсенберг С.А., Современные мараны, *Еврейская неделя*, №14-15, 1916, с. 78-84.

Valikhanov, 1986
Валиханов Ч.Ч., *Избранные произведения*, Москва, 1986.

Vambery, 1864
Vambery A., *Travels in Central Asia*, London, 1864.

Vambery, 1876
Vambery H., *Sittenbilder aus dem Morgenlande*, Berlin, 1876.

Venyukov, 1877
Венюков М.И., Поступательное движение России в Средней Азии, *Сборник государственных знаний*, том 3, С. Петербург, 1877, с. 58-106.

Verman, 1991
ד. ורמן, הבוכארים ושכונתם בירושלים, ירושלים, 1991

Vlasov, 1894
Власов П.М., Статистические сведения о Дерегазском, Кучанском, Буджкурдском и Келатском округах Хоросана,

Сборник географических, топографических и статистических материалов по Азии, выпуск 56, С. Петербург, 1894, с. 126-175.

Von der Hoffen, 1900
фон-дер-Ховен Н., О среднеазиатских евреях, *Будущность,* №23, 09.06.1900, с. 468-470; №26, 30.06.1900, с. 530-531; №36, 08.09.1900, с. 733-735.

Voskhod, 1889
Недельная хроника Восхода, №32, 13.08.1889, с. 818.
Voskhod, 1902
Восход, №48, 28.11.1902, с. 19.
Voskhod, 1904
Восход, №1, 09.01.1904, с. 16-17.

Vremennoe polozhenie, 1911
Временное положение об управлении Закаспийской области, издание 1892 г., составитель А.Л. Саатчиан, *Полный свод законов Российской империи,* том II, С. Петербург, 1911, с. 941-946.

Weissenberg, 1913
Weissenberg S., *Die zentralasiatischen Juden in anthropologischer Beziehung,* Wien, 1913.

Wolff, 1837
Wolff J., *Researches and Missionary Labours among the Jews, Mohammedans and other sects,* 2 education, 1 American education, revised and corrected by the author, Philadelphia, 1837.

Wolff, 1846
Wolff J., *Narrative of a mission to Bokhara in the years 1843-1845,* 5 ed., London, 1846.

Wolff, 1860-1861

Wolff J., *Travels and Adventures of the rev. Joseph Wolff*, 2 ed., vol. 1-2, London, 1860-1861.

Zand, 1977

מ. זנד, יהדות בוכרה, בתוך ח. אשרוב, <u>מסמרקנד עד פתח-</u><u>תקוה</u>, תל-אביב, 1977, עמ' 161-165.

Zand, 1988

מ. זנד, התיישבות היהודים באסיה התיכונה בימי קדם ובימי הביניים המוקדמים, <u>פעמים</u>, גל' 35, 1988, עמ' 4 - 23.

Zand, 1990

Zand M., Bukharan Jews, *Encyclopedia Iranica*, vol. 4, London - New-York, 1990, pp. 530-545.

Zashchuk, 1928

Защук С., Торговля Средней Азии с сопредельными странами Востока, *Новый Восток*, №20-21, 1928, с. 218-240.

Bei Fragen zur Produktsicherheit wenden Sie sich bitte an:
If you have any questions regarding product safety,
please contact:

Walter de Gruyter GmbH
Genthiner Straße 13
10785 Berlin
productsafety@degruyterbrill.com